FRACTURED LANDS

BY SCOTT ANDERSON
PHOTOGRAPHS BY PAOLO PELLEGRIN

This project was made possible in part by a generous grant from the Pulitzer Center, which supports global journalism and education.

On Aug. 14, 2016, The New York Times Magazine published an unusual issue. It contained just one story, a 42,000-word narrative titled, "Fractured Lands," written by Scott Anderson, with photographs by Paolo Pellegrin. The product of some 18 months of reporting, Anderson and Pellegrin's story examined the unraveling of the Arab world since the United States invaded Iraq in 2003, a catastrophe that helped lead to the collapse of regimes throughout the Middle East, the rise of ISIS and an ongoing global refugee crisis. Seen through the eyes of six characters in Egypt, Libya, Syria, Iraq and Iraqi Kurdistan, "Fractured Lands" took a bewildering crisis and made it comprehensible. The issue became an instant classic. Many readers sent letters saying that it helped them to finally understand, with vivid clarity, the central conflict of our time.

This special hardcover edition contains the story as it was originally published, along with 15 additional images not seen in the Aug. 14 issue. "Fractured Lands" was an unusual magazine story not only for its length, for the depth of its reporting or for the novelistic sweep of its storytelling, but also because, in its determination to offer a full and humanistic explanation of this crisis, it transcended the news cycle and offered something of truly lasting value. We now present it to you in a truly lasting format.

Jake Silverstein, Editor in Chief
The New York Times Magazine

December 2016

PRINCIPAL CHARACTERS

LIBYA

Majdi el-Mangoush, 30. An air force cadet with divided loyalties.

EGYPT

Laila Soueif, 60. The matriarch of a prominent dissident family.

SYRIA

Majd Ibrahim, 24. A college student caught in Syria's "Stalingrad."

Illustrations by Louise Zergaeng Pomeroy

IRAQ

Wakaz Hassan, 22. A day laborer recruited by ISIS.

Azar Mirkhan, 41. A Kurdish doctor on leave to battle ISIS.

Khulood al-Zaidi, 36. A women's rights activist targeted by militias.

TURKEY

PAKISTAN

Kurdistan Regional Government

Sinjar

Mosul   Erbil

Kirkuk

IRAN

Tikrit

Aleppo   Raqqa

SYRIA

Baghdad

Falluja

Homs

IRAQ

Kut

CYPRUS

Basra

Damascus

LEBANON

KUWAIT

Arabian Sea

ISRAEL

Amman

Persian Gulf

JORDAN

U.A.E.

Cairo

OMAN

SAUDI ARABIA

EGYPT

Red Sea

YEMEN

Indian Ocean

SUDAN

ERITREA

PREFACE

BEFORE DRIVING INTO northern Iraq, Dr. Azar Mirkhan changed from his Western clothes into the traditional dress of a Kurdish pesh merga warrior: a tightfitting short woolen jacket over his shirt, baggy pantaloons and a wide cummerbund. He also thought to bring along certain accessories. These included a combat knife, tucked neatly into the waist of his cummerbund, as well as sniper binoculars and a loaded .45 semiautomatic. Should matters turn particularly ticklish, an M-4 assault rifle lay within easy reach on the back seat, with extra clips in the foot well. The doctor shrugged. "It's a bad neighborhood."

Our destination that day in May 2015 was the place of Azar's greatest sorrow, one that haunted him still. The previous year, ISIS gunmen had cut a murderous swath through northern Iraq, brushing away an Iraqi Army vastly greater in size, and then turning their attention to the Kurds. Azar had divined precisely where the ISIS killers were about to strike, knew that tens of thousands of civilians stood helpless in their path, but had been unable to get anyone to heed his warnings. In desperation, he had loaded up his car with guns and raced to the scene, only to come to a spot in the road where he saw he was just hours too late. "It was obvious," Azar said, "so obvious. But no one wanted to listen." On that day, we were returning to the place where the fabled Kurdish warriors of northern Iraq had been outmaneuvered and put to flight, where Dr. Azar Mirkhan had failed to avert a colossal tragedy — and where, for many more months to come, he would continue to battle ISIS.

Azar is a practicing urologist, but even without the firepower and warrior get-up, the 41-year-old would exude the aura of a hunter. He walks with a curious loping gait that produces little sound, and

in conversation has a tendency to tuck his chin and stare from beneath heavy-lidded eyes, rather as if he were sighting down a gun. With his prominent nose and jet black pompadour, he bears a passing resemblance to a young Johnny Cash.

The weaponry also complemented the doctor's personal philosophy, as expressed in a scene from one of his favorite movies, "The Good, the Bad and the Ugly," when a bathing Eli Wallach is caught off guard by a man seeking to kill him. Rather than immediately shoot Wallach, the would-be assassin goes into a triumphant soliloquy, allowing Wallach to kill him first.

"When you have to shoot, shoot; don't talk," Azar quoted from the movie. "That is us Kurds now. This is not the time to talk, but to shoot."

AZAR IS ONE of six people whose lives are chronicled in these pages. The six are from different regions, different cities, different tribes, different families, but they share, along with millions of other people in and from the Middle East, an experience of profound unraveling. Their lives have been forever altered by upheavals that began in 2003 with the American invasion of Iraq, and then accelerated with the series of revolutions and insurrections that have collectively become known in the West as the Arab Spring. They continue today with the depredations of ISIS, with terrorist attacks and with failing states.

For each of these six people, the upheavals were crystallized by a specific, singular event. For Azar Mirkhan, it came on the road to Sinjar, when he saw that his worst fears had come true. For Laila Soueif in Egypt, it came when a young man separated from a sprinting mass of protesters to embrace her, and she thought she knew the revolution would succeed. For Majdi el-Mangoush

in Libya, it came as he walked across a deadly no-man's-land and, overwhelmed by a sudden euphoria, felt free for the first time in his life. For Khulood al-Zaidi in Iraq, it came when, with just a few menacing words from a former friend, she finally understood that everything she had worked for was gone. For Majd Ibrahim in Syria, it came when, watching an interrogator search his cellphone for the identity of his "controller," he knew his own execution was drawing nearer by the moment. For Wakaz Hassan in Iraq, a young man with no apparent interest in politics or religion, it came on the day ISIS gunmen showed up in his village and offered him a choice.

As disparate as those moments were, for each of these six people they represented a crossing over, passage to a place from which there will never be a return. Such changes, of course — multiplied by millions of lives — are also transforming their homelands, the greater Middle East and, by inevitable extension, the entire world.

HISTORY NEVER FLOWS in a predictable way. It is always a result of seemingly random currents and incidents, the significance of which can be determined — or, more often, disputed — only in hindsight. But even accounting for history's capricious nature, the event credited with setting off the Arab Spring could hardly have been more improbable: the suicide by immolation of a poor Tunisian fruit-and-vegetable seller in protest over government harassment. By the time Mohamed Bouazizi succumbed to his injuries on Jan. 4, 2011, the protesters who initially took to Tunisia's streets calling for economic reform were demanding the resignation of Zine el-Abidine Ben Ali, the nation's strongman president for 23 years. In subsequent days, those demonstrations grew in size and intensity — and then they jumped Tunisia's border. By the end of January, anti-government protests had erupted in Algeria, Egypt, Oman and Jordan. That was only the beginning. By November, just 10 months after Bouazizi's death, four longstanding Middle Eastern dictatorships had been toppled, a half-dozen other suddenly embattled governments had undergone shake-ups or had promised reforms, and anti-government demonstrations — some peaceful, others violent — had spread in an arc across the Arab world from Mauritania to Bahrain.

As a writer with long experience in the Middle East, I initially welcomed the convulsions of the Arab Spring — indeed, I believed they were long overdue. In the early 1970s, I traveled through the region as a young boy with my father, a journey that sparked both my fascination with Islam and my love of the desert. The Middle East was also the site of my first foray into journalism when, in the summer of 1983, I hopped on a plane to the embattled city Beirut in hopes of finding work as a stringer. Over the subsequent years, I embedded with a platoon of Israeli commandos conducting raids in the West Bank; dined with Janjaweed raiders in Darfur; interviewed the families of suicide bombers. Ultimately, I took a five-year hiatus from magazine journalism to write a book on the historical origins of the modern Middle East.

In my professional travels over the decades, I had found no other region to rival the Arab world in its utter stagnation. While Muammar el-Qaddafi of Libya set a record for longevity in the Middle East with his 42-year dictatorship, it was not that different elsewhere; by 2011, any Egyptian younger than 41 — and that was roughly 75 percent of the population — had only ever known two heads of state, while a Syrian of the same age had

lived his or her entire life under the control of the father-and-son Assad dynasty. Along with political stasis, in many Arab nations most levers of economic power lay in the hands of small oligarchies or aristocratic families; for everyone else, about the only path to financial security was to wrangle a job within fantastically bloated public-sector bureaucracies, government agencies that were often themselves monuments to nepotism and corruption. While the sheer amount of money pouring into oil-rich, sparsely populated nations like Libya or Kuwait might allow for a degree of economic trickle-down prosperity, this was not the case in more populous but resource-poor nations like Egypt or Syria, where poverty and underemployment were severe and — given the ongoing regional population explosion — ever-worsening problems.

I was heartened, in the Arab Spring's early days, by the focus of the people's wrath. One of the Arab world's most prominent and debilitating features, I had long felt, was a culture of grievance that was defined less by what people aspired to than by what they opposed. They were anti-Zionist, anti-West, anti-imperialist. For generations, the region's dictators had been adroit at channeling public frustration toward these external "enemies" and away from their own misrule. But with the Arab Spring, that old playbook suddenly didn't work anymore. Instead, and for the first time on such a mass scale, the people of the Middle East were directing their rage squarely at the regimes themselves.

Then it all went horribly wrong. By the summer of 2012, two of the "freed" nations — Libya and Yemen — were sliding into anarchy and factionalism, while the struggle against the Bashar al-Assad government in Syria had descended into vicious

civil war. In Egypt the following summer, the nation's first democratically elected government was overthrown by the military, a coup cheered on by many of the same young activists who took to the streets to demand democracy two years earlier. The only truly bright spot among the Arab Spring nations was the place where it started, Tunisia, but even there, terrorist attacks and feuding politicians were a constant threat to a fragile government. Amid the chaos, the remnants of Osama bin Laden's old outfit, Al Qaeda, gained a new lease on life, resurrected the war in Iraq and then spawned an even more severe and murderous offshoot: the Islamic State, or ISIS.

WHY DID IT turn out this way? Why did a movement begun with such high promise go so terribly awry?

The scattershot nature of the Arab Spring makes it hard to provide a single answer. Some nations were radically transformed, even as others right next door were barely touched. Some of the nations in crisis were relatively wealthy (Libya), others crushingly poor (Yemen). Some countries with comparatively benign dictatorships (Tunisia) blew up along with some of the region's most brutal (Syria). The same range of political and economic disparity is seen in the nations that remained stable.

Yet one pattern does emerge, and it is striking. While most of the 22 nations that make up the Arab world have been buffeted to some degree by the Arab Spring, the six most profoundly affected — Egypt, Iraq, Libya, Syria, Tunisia and Yemen — are all republics, rather than monarchies. And of these six, the three that have disintegrated so completely as to raise doubt that they will ever again exist as functioning states — Iraq, Syria and

Libya — are all members of that small list of Arab countries created by Western imperial powers in the early 20th century. In each, little thought was given to national coherence, and even less to tribal or sectarian divisions. Certainly, these same internal divisions exist in many of the region's other republics, as well as in its monarchies, but it would seem undeniable that those two factors operating in concert — the lack of an intrinsic sense of national identity joined to a form of government that supplanted the traditional organizing principle of society — left Iraq, Syria and Libya especially vulnerable when the storms of change descended.

In fact, all but one of the six people profiled ahead are from these "artificial states," and their individual stories are rooted in the larger story of how those nations came to be. The process began at the end of World War I, when two of the victorious allies, Britain and France, carved up the lands of the defeated Ottoman Empire between themselves as spoils of war. In Mesopotamia, the British joined together three largely autonomous Ottoman provinces and named it Iraq. The southernmost of these provinces was dominated by Shiite Arabs, the central by Sunni Arabs and the northernmost by non-Arab Kurds. To the west of Iraq, the European powers took the opposite approach, carving the vast lands of "greater Syria" into smaller, more manageable parcels. Falling under French rule was the smaller rump state of Syria — essentially the nation that exists today — and the coastal enclave of Lebanon, while the British took Palestine and Transjordan, a swath of southern Syria that would eventually become Israel and Jordan. Coming a bit later to the game, in 1934, Italy joined the three ancient North African regions that it had wrested from the Ottomans in 1912 to form the colony of Libya.

To maintain dominion over these fractious territories, the European powers adopted the same divide-and-conquer approach that served them so well in the colonization of sub-Saharan Africa. This consisted of empowering a local ethnic or religious minority to serve as their local administrators, confident that this minority would never rebel against their foreign overseers lest they be engulfed by the disenfranchised majority.

This was only the most overt level of the Europeans' divide-and-conquer strategy, however, for just beneath the sectarian and regional divisions in these "nations" there lay extraordinarily complex tapestries of tribes and subtribes and clans, ancient social orders that remained the populations' principal source of identification and allegiance. Much as the United States Army and white settlers did with Indian tribes in the conquest of the American West, so the British and French and Italians proved adept at pitting these groups against one another, bestowing favors — weapons or food or sinecures — to one faction in return for fighting another. The great difference, of course, is that in the American West, the settlers stayed and the tribal system was essentially destroyed. In the Arab world, the Europeans eventually left, but the sectarian and tribal schisms they fueled remained.

SEEN IN THIS light, the 2011 suicide of Mohamed Bouazizi seems less the catalyst for the Arab Spring than a culmination of tensions and contradictions that had been simmering under the surface of Arab society for a long time. Indeed, throughout the Arab world, residents are far more likely to point to a different event, one that occurred eight years before Bouazizi's death, as the moment when the process of disintegration began: the American invasion of Iraq. Many even point to a singular image that embodied that upheaval. It came on the afternoon of April 9, 2003, in the Firdos Square of downtown Baghdad, when, with the help of a winch and an American M88 armored recovery vehicle, a towering statue of the Iraqi dictator, Saddam Hussein, was pulled to the ground.

While today that image is remembered in the Arab world with resentment — the symbolism of this latest Western intervention in their region was quite inescapable — at the time it spurred something far more nuanced. For the first time in their lives, what Syrians and Libyans and other Arabs just as much as Iraqis saw was that a figure as seemingly immovable as Saddam Hussein could be cast aside, that the political and social paralysis that had so long held their collective lands might actually be broken. Not nearly so apparent was that these strongmen had actually exerted considerable energy to bind up their nations, and in their absence the ancient forces of tribalism and sectarianism would begin to exert their own centrifugal pull. Even less apparent was how these forces would both attract and repel the United States, damaging its power and prestige in the region to an extent from which it might never recover.

At least one man saw this quite clearly. For much of 2002, the Bush administration had laid the groundwork for the Iraq invasion by accusing Saddam Hussein of pursuing a weapons-of-mass-destruction program and obliquely linking him to the Sept. 11 attacks. In October 2002, six months before Firdos Square, I had a long interview with Muammar el-Qaddafi, and I asked him who would benefit if the Iraq invasion actually occurred. The Libyan dictator had a habit of theatrically pondering before answering my questions, but his reply to that one was instantaneous. "Bin Laden," he said. "There is no doubt about that. And Iraq could end up becoming the staging ground for Al Qaeda, because if the Saddam government collapses, it will be anarchy in Iraq. If that happens, actions against Americans will be considered jihad."

BEGINNING IN APRIL 2015, the photographer Paolo Pellegrin and I embarked on a series of extended trips to the Middle East. Separately and as a writer-photographer team, we had covered an array of conflicts in the region over the previous 20 years, and our hope on this new set of journeys was to gain a greater understanding of the so-called Arab Spring and its generally grim aftermath. As the situation continued to deteriorate through 2015 and 2016, our travels expanded: to those islands in Greece bearing the brunt of the migrant exodus from Iraq and Syria; to the front lines in northern Iraq where the battle against ISIS was being most vigorously waged.

We have presented the results of this 16-month project in the form of six individual narratives, which, woven within the larger strands of history, aim to provide a tapestry of an Arab World in revolt.

The account is divided into five parts, which proceed chronologically as they alternate between our principal characters. Along with introducing several of these individuals, Part 1 focuses on three historical factors that are crucial to understanding the current crisis: the inherent instability of the Middle East's artificial states; the precarious position in which U.S.-allied Arab governments have found themselves when compelled to pursue policies bitterly opposed by their own people; and American involvement in the de facto partitioning of Iraq 25 years ago, an event little remarked upon at the time — and barely more so since — that helped call into question the very legitimacy of the modern Arab nation-state. Part 2 is primarily devoted to the American invasion of Iraq, and to how it laid the groundwork for the Arab Spring revolts. In Part 3, the narrative quickens, as we follow the explosive outcome of those revolts as they occurred in Egypt, Libya and Syria. By Part 4, which chronicles the rise of ISIS, and Part 5, which tracks the resulting exodus from the region, we are squarely in the present, at the heart of the world's gravest concern.

I have tried to tell a human story, one that has its share of heroes, even some glimmers of hope. But what follows, ultimately, is a dark warning. Today the tragedy and violence of the Middle East have spilled from its banks, with nearly a million Syrians and Iraqis flooding into Europe to escape the wars in their homelands, and terrorist attacks in Dhaka, Paris and beyond. With the ISIS cause being invoked by mass murderers in San Bernardino and Orlando, the issues of immigration and terrorism have now become conjoined in many Americans' minds, forming a key political flash point in the coming presidential election. In some sense, it is fitting that the crisis of the Arab world has its roots in the First World War, for like that war, it is a regional crisis that has come quickly and widely — with little seeming reason or logic — to influence events at every corner of the globe. ◆

PART I:
ORIGINS

1.

Laila Soueif
Egypt

LAILA SOUEIF attended her first political rally when she was just 16. It was 1972, and the protesters were demanding what students have so often desired — a more equitable world, greater freedom of expression. But they also had a demand that was a bit more specific to the Arab world: that Egypt's president, Anwar Sadat, launch a war to recover the Sinai Peninsula, which was seized by Israel in the Six-Day War of 1967. From this experience, Laila would soon be convinced of the power of civil disobedience; Sadat launched an attack on Israel the following year. What Laila hadn't counted on was the more immediate wrath of her parents. Just two hours after she joined the protest in Cairo's Tahrir Square, Laila's mother and father tracked down their teenage daughter and dragged her home. "From that, I learned that it was easier to defy the state than to defy my parents," she said.

Laila was born into a life of both privilege and intellectual freedom. Her parents were college professors, and her older sister, Ahdaf Soueif, is one of Egypt's best-known contemporary novelists. She gravitated toward leftist politics at an early age. While studying mathematics at Cairo University in the mid-1970s, she met her future husband, Ahmed Seif, who was already the leader of an underground communist student cell calling for revolution.

By then, Egypt had long been regarded as the political capital of the Middle East, the birthplace of revolutionary movements and ideas. In the modern era, it owed that status largely to the legacy of one man: Gamal Abdel Nasser.

Well into the 1940s, Egypt, along with most of the rest of the Middle East, remained a lesser global concern, still in the thrall of the European powers that imposed their will on the area decades before. That began to change at the end of World War II with the discovery of vast new oil fields in the region, and with the collapse of the British and French colonial empires. The pace of change greatly accelerated when Nasser and his Free Officers Movement of junior military officers overthrew Egypt's Western-pliant king in 1952.

Championing "Arab socialism" and Pan-Arab unity, Nasser swiftly became a galvanizing figure throughout the Arab world, the spokesman for a people long dominated by foreigners and Western-educated elites. Just as crucial to the strongman's popularity was what he opposed: colonialism, imperialism and that most immediate and enduring example of the West's meddling in the region, the state of Israel.

Nasser's success inspired many other would-be Arab leaders, nowhere more so than in the artificial states of the Middle East formed by the European powers. By 1968, military officers espousing the Baathist ("renaissance") philosophy — a quasi-socialist form of Pan-Arabism — had seized power in Iraq and Syria. They were joined the following year by the Libyan lieutenant Muammar el-Qaddafi, and his somewhat-baffling "third universal theory," which rejected traditional democracy in favor of rule by "people's committees." In all three countries, just as in Egypt, Western-favored monarchs or Parliaments were neutered or cast aside.

But Nasser possessed an advantage that his fellow autocrats in the region did not. With a sense of national identity that stretched back millenniums, Egypt never seemed in danger of being torn apart; the centrifugal pull of tribes or clans or sectarian identity simply didn't exist there to the degree it did in Syria or Iraq. At the same time, Egypt's long tradition of relative liberalism had given rise to a fractious political landscape that ran the spectrum from secular communists to fundamentalist Islamists.

Part of Nasser's genius was his ability to bridge these divides, and he did so by appealing both to Egyptian national pride and to a shared antipathy for the West, a vestige, perhaps, of 70 years of heavy-handed rule by Britain. Thus, even when Islamist conservatives became alarmed by Nasser's moves toward greater secularism, most still saw him as a hero for nationalizing Western businesses, and for besting Britain, France and Israel in the 1956 Suez crisis. Similarly, urban liberals like the Soueif family who disdained Nasser's strong-arm rule — his was a military dictatorship, after all — also cheered him for his leadership in the international Nonaligned Movement, for proudly thumbing his nose at the threats and enticements of the United States as it sought to compel Egypt into its orbit during the Cold War. This became the means by which Nasser and his successor, Anwar Sadat, maintained their grip on power: play left and right off each other as a matter of course; bring them together when needed by focusing on an external foe. Such maneuvering resulted in many odd political turns, including the first protest march of Laila Soueif.

After working on leftist causes together throughout their time at the University of Cairo, Laila and Ahmed married in 1978. That same year, Egypt's political landscape was neatly turned upside down. In September, Sadat signed the Camp David accords, which led to an American-brokered peace treaty with Israel. That stunning about-face simultaneously propelled Egypt into the camp of American client-states and isolated it from much of the rest of the Arab world. Even more ominously for Sadat, what was

seen in the West as an act of courage was regarded by most Egyptians as an act of betrayal and national shame. This was certainly the view of Laila and Ahmed. It was in the wake of the 1979 peace treaty that some of the men in Ahmed's underground cell began buying up arms on the black market and vowing armed action against the government. Those plans never got off the ground, though. Instead, it was a cabal of Islamist military plotters who finally got to Sadat, shooting and killing him at a military parade in Cairo in October 1981.

A month later, Laila gave birth to her and Ahmed's first child, a boy they named Alaa. Their lives took on an air of increasingly apolitical domesticity, and by 1983, Laila, then 28, was juggling the demands of child-rearing with her new position as a professor of mathematics at Cairo University. All normalcy was shattered, however, when Sadat's successor, Hosni Mubarak, ordered a sweeping security crackdown. Among those ensnared in the dragnet were Ahmed and his colleagues in the underground cell. Severely tortured until he signed a full confession, Ahmed was then released to await his verdict. When that verdict was returned, in late 1984, the news was grim: Ahmed was found guilty of illegal weapons possession and sentenced to five years in prison.

At the time, Laila was in France, having accepted a scholarship to further her math studies, but when Ahmed's sentence was handed down, she rushed back to Cairo with Alaa. Thanks to a curious loophole in Egyptian law, sentences for security-related offenses like Ahmed's had to be approved by the president, a process that normally took several months and during which the defendant could remain out on bail. It presented the couple with a tempting choice.

"We had to decide," Laila, who is now 60, told me. "Does he submit and go into prison for five years, do we try to find some way to get him out of the country or do we go into hiding?" She gave a nonchalant shrug. "So we went into hiding."

For several months, the couple lived as fugitives with their 3-year-old son. Ultimately, though, both realized it was a futile exercise. "He wasn't willing to leave the country," Laila said, "and he couldn't stay in hiding forever. He decided it was easier to do the five years, so he gave himself up." But not necessarily easier for Laila. She became pregnant during her and Ahmed's brief time on the run, leaving her to tend to a second child, a girl they named Mona, as Ahmed served out his prison sentence.

It was in prison that Ahmed experienced something of an epiphany. By continuing the entente with the United States and Israel that Sadat had begun, Mubarak naturally also inherited the taint of capitulation in the eyes of many of his countrymen. Unable to forge national cohesion by turning to the old external enemy card — after all, Egypt was now in bed with those supposed enemies — Mubarak had devised a more carefully calibrated system to play his secular leftist and militant Islamist oppositions against each other. Ahmed, thrown into prison with both factions, saw firsthand how this strategy played out when it came to even the most basic of human rights. As he would later tell Joe Stork of Human Rights Watch, "The communists would say secretly, 'It doesn't matter if Islamists are tortured.' And the Islamists would say, 'Why not torture communists?'"

Determined to fight for judicial reform, Ahmed devoted himself to studying law in his prison cell. Within a month of his release in 1989, he was admitted to the Egyptian bar.

This placed the ex-political prisoner and his wife at a crossroads. With Laila a tenured professor at Cairo University and Ahmed now a lawyer, the couple had the opportunity to carve out a comfortable existence for themselves among the Cairene elite. Instead, and at ultimately great personal cost, they would plunge ever deeper into Egypt's widening turmoils, trying to cross the very divides that had for so long been critical to the government's own survival.

2.

Majdi el-Mangoush
Libya

A ONCE-PROSPEROUS port city roughly 120 miles east of Tripoli, the Libyan capital, Misurata was a main terminus of the old trans-Saharan trade route, the stopping point of camel caravans taking gold and slaves from sub-Saharan Africa for export across the Mediterranean. Ever since, it has been one of Libya's chief commercial hubs, its residents regarded as industrious and particularly capitalist-minded. Prominent among those inhabitants is the Mangoush clan, so much so that one of the oldest neighborhoods of the city bears the family name. And it was in that neighborhood on July 4, 1986, that Omar and Fatheya el-Mangoush, civil servants for the Misurata municipal government, welcomed the birth of the youngest of their six children, a boy they named Majdi.

By the time of Majdi's birth, Libya had been ruled by Muammar el-Qaddafi for 17 years.

Viewed in the West as something of a rakish *enfant terrible* when he and his fellow military plotters overthrew Libya's king in 1969 — Qaddafi was then himself just 27 — the handsome former signal corps lieutenant was wildly popular among his countrymen in the years immediately following the coup. A key to that popularity was his emulation of Gamal Abdel Nasser in neighboring Egypt. Like Nasser, Qaddafi kindled Arab pride by nationalizing Western business interests, including parts of Libya's vital oil industry, and standing in vehement opposition to the state of Israel. By spreading the wealth around, he also enabled families like the Mangoushes to live a comfortable middle-class life.

Over time, however, Qaddafi's rule increasingly bore less resemblance to Egypt's "soft" dictatorship and more to that of two others influenced by the Nasser model: the Baathist regimes of Saddam Hussein in Iraq and Hafez al-Assad in Syria. The parallels were quite striking. In all three countries, the dictators developed elaborate personality cults — their faces adorned posters and murals and postage stamps — and aligned themselves with the "anti-imperialist" bloc of Arab nations, their stances helped along by deepening ties with the Soviet Union. True to the Baathist credo of "Arab socialism" and Qaddafi's third universal theory, all three countries embarked on fabulously ambitious public works projects, building hospitals and schools and colleges throughout their lands and bankrolling those enterprises with oil receipts (in the cases of Libya and Iraq), or through the patronage of the Soviet Union (in the case of Syria). At the same time, the states established extravagantly bloated governmental structures, such that their ministries and agencies quickly became the main pillars of the economy; eventually more than half of the Libyan work force — Majdi el-Mangoush's parents among them — was on the government payroll, and the figures in Saddam Hussein's Iraq were similar. "Everybody was connected to the state somehow," Majdi explained. "For their housing, for their job. It was impossible to exist outside of it."

For all their revolutionary rhetoric, the dictators of Libya, Iraq and Syria remained ever mindful that their nations were essentially artificial constructs. What this meant was that many of their subjects' primary loyalty lay not to the state but to their tribe or, more broadly, to their ethnic group or religious sect. To keep them loyal required both the carrot and the stick. In all three nations, the leaders entered into elaborate and labyrinthine alliances with various tribes and clans. Stay on the dictator's good side, and your tribe might be given control of a ministry or a lucrative business concession; fall on his bad side, and you're all out in the cold. The strongmen also carefully forged ties across ethnic and religious divides. In Iraq, even though most all senior Baathist officials were, like Saddam Hussein, of the Sunni minority, he endeavored to sprinkle just enough Shiites and Kurds through his administration to lend it an ecumenical sheen. In Hafez al-Assad's Sunni-majority Syria, rule by his Alawite minority was augmented by a de facto alliance with the nation's Christian community, giving another significant minority a stake in the status quo.

This coalition-building had a unique geographic dimension in Libya. Aside from the historical rivalry that existed between the principal regions, Tripolitania and Cyrenaica, human settlement in Libya had always been clustered along the Mediterranean coast, and what developed there over the millenniums was essentially a series of semiautonomous city-states that resisted central rule. Thus, while Qaddafi didn't need to worry about religious sectarianism — virtually all Libyans are Sunni Muslims — he did need to think about drawing into his ruling circle the requisite number of Misuratans and Benghazians to keep everyone mollified.

And if inducements and handshakes didn't work, there was always the stick. Libya, Iraq

and Syria erected some of the most brutal and ubiquitous state security apparatuses to be found in the world. Operating with utter impunity, the local security forces, or *mukhabarat,* of all three dictatorships rounded up enemies of the state, real or imagined, at will, to be thrown into their nation's dungeons after sham trials or simply executed on the spot. The repression wasn't limited to individuals but often extended to entire tribes or ethnic groups. Certainly the most notorious case was Saddam Hussein's Anfal campaign against Iraq's ever-restive Kurdish minority in 1988; before that pogrom was over, between 50,000 and 100,000 Kurds had been killed. Over a two-year period, hundreds of thousands more were turned out of their razed villages and forcibly relocated.

The state also had a very long memory, as Majdi el-Mangoush discovered growing up in Misurata. In 1975, two of his mother's relatives, both midlevel army officers, joined in a failed coup attempt against Qaddafi. While both were executed, that didn't remove the stain on the family name. (Testament to the enduring tribal nature of Libya, Majdi's mother was also of the Mangoush clan.)

"It's not that we were directly persecuted because of it," Majdi, who is now 30, explained, "but it was something officials would always comment on: 'Ah, so you're a Mangoush.' It meant the government watched you a little closer, that you were never viewed as completely trustworthy."

And in all three countries, there dwelled one group that was deemed wholly untrustworthy, one that almost always received the stick: Islamic fundamentalists. In Syria and Iraq, even identifying oneself as a Sunni or Shia could draw state suspicion, and in all three nations the *mukhabarat* had a special brief to surveil conservative clerics and religious agitators. Subtlety was not a hallmark of these campaigns. When, in February 1982, a group of Sunni fundamentalists in Syria under the Muslim Brotherhood banner seized control of portions of the city Hama, Hafez al-Assad had the place encircled with ground troops and tanks and artillery. In the ensuing three-week "Hama massacre," somewhere between 10,000 and 40,000 residents were killed.

But a perverse dynamic often takes hold in strongman dictators — and here, too, there were great similarities among Qaddafi, Hussein and Assad. Part of it stems from what might be called the naked-emperor syndrome, whereby, in the constant company of sycophants, the leader gradually becomes unmoored from reality. Another is rooted in the very nature of a police state. The greater the repression of security forces, the further that any true dissent burrows underground, making it that much harder for a dictator to know where his actual enemies are;

this fuels a deepening state of paranoia, which can be assuaged only through even greater repression. By the 1990s, this cycle had produced a bizarre contradiction in Iraq, Syria and Libya: The more the leaders promoted a cult of hero worship and wallpapered their nations with their likenesses, the more reclusive those leaders became. In Majdi el-Mangoush's case, despite living in a country whose total population was less than that of New York's five boroughs, not once in 25 years did he ever personally glimpse Qaddafi. This was about the same number of times he uttered the dictator's name in a disparaging way in public. "You would only do that with family, or with the most trusted of friends," Majdi explained. "If you were around others and wanted to say something at all critical, it was 'our friend.'"

There was another notable aspect to the posters and murals and mosaics of the dictators that could be seen everywhere in Libya, Iraq and Syria. In a great many of them, framing the image of the strongman, there appeared the outline of the country's borders. Perhaps that juxtaposition was designed to impart a simple message — "I am the leader of the nation" — but it's possible that the artificial-state dictators were also sending a message that was both more ambitious and more admonishing: "I am the nation; and if I go, then so goes the nation." Of course, that may have been just what many members of the Mangoush clan — celebrated enough to have their own namesake neighborhood, notorious enough to be permanently marked — were secretly hoping.

3.

Azar Mirkhan
Kurdistan

IN EARLY 1975, as Laila Soueif, at Cairo University, continued to agitate for change, Gen. Heso Mirkhan was serving as a chief lieutenant to Mustafa Barzani, the legendary warlord of the Iraqi Kurds, in a brutal guerrilla war against the Baathist government in Baghdad. For more than a year, the vastly outnumbered Kurdish fighters, known as the pesh merga, had fought the Iraqi Army to a standstill. Crucial to the Kurds' success was a steady flow of C.I.A.-supplied weaponry, along with Iranian military advisers, as Iran waged a U.S.-sponsored proxy war against Iraq. But when the shah of Iran and Saddam Hussein abruptly concluded a peace treaty in early March, Secretary of State Henry Kissinger ordered an immediate cutoff of aid to the Kurds. In the face of an all-out Iraqi offensive, Barzani was airlifted out to end his days in a C.I.A. safe house in Northern Virginia, but thousands of other stranded pesh merga fighters were left to their fate, including Heso Mirkhan. With Saddam Hussein's soldiers closing in, the general led his family in a frantic dash over the mountains for sanctuary in Iran. Somewhere along the way, his wife gave birth to another son.

"The treaty was signed on the 6th of March," Azar Mirkhan, who is now 41, explained, "and I was born on the 7th. My mother gave birth to me on the road, on the border between Iran and Iraq." He gave a rueful little laugh. "That is why my family has always called me 'the lucky child.' Kurdish luck."

Indeed, it is hard to find any people quite as unlucky as the Kurds. Spread across the mountainous reaches of four nations — Iraq, Iran, Syria and Turkey — they have always regarded themselves as culturally apart from their neighbors and have constantly battled for independence from those nations they inhabit. The governments of these nations have tended to view their reluctant Kurdish subjects with both fear and distrust, and have taken turns quashing their bids for independence. Those governments have also periodically employed the Kurds — either

their own or those of their neighbors — as proxy fighters to attack or unsettle their regional enemies-of-the-day. Historically, when those feuds were brought to an end, so, too, was the Kurds' usefulness, and they were soon abandoned — as occurred in the 1975 "great betrayal."

While the number of rebellions and proxy wars that have occurred across the breadth of Kurdistan over the past century is almost impossible to count, the biography of Heso Mirkhan's commander, Mustafa Barzani, provides something of a gauge. By the time of his death in 1979, the 75-year-old Barzani had not only waged war against Turkey, Iran (twice) and the central government of Iraq (four times), but had somehow found the energy to also take it to the Ottomans and the British and a host of Kurdish rivals. Multiply Barzani's list by four — the Kurds of Syria, Iran and Turkey have each had their own competing guerrilla groups and independence movements — and it all becomes a bit staggering.

Despite the fears of these governments that they might some day be confronted by an independent "greater Kurdistan," the truth is that the differences among the Kurds in these four

countries now rival their similarities. One thing they have in common, though, is a longstanding warrior tradition, and among the Kurds of northern Iraq, there is no more celebrated family of pesh merga — literally translated as "those who face death" — than the Mirkhans.

Following their father, Dr. Azar Mirkhan and four of his nine brothers have undergone pesh merga training; today, one brother, Araz, is a senior pesh merga commander on the front lines. But the family has paid a high price for membership in the warrior caste. Heso, the patriarch, was killed in combat in 1983, while one of Azar's older brothers, Ali, met the same end in 1994.

But it hasn't been just the region's governments that have historically victimized the Kurds. In fact, few nations have brought the Kurds of northern Iraq more sorrow than the United States. After their role in the great betrayal of 1975, the Americans would again be complicit in the Kurds' suffering — if this time largely through silence — just 10 years later.

By then, the United States' chief ally in the region, the shah of Iran, had been overthrown and replaced by the hostile Shiite fundamentalist government of Ayatollah Khomeini. Searching for a new partner in the region, Washington found one in Saddam Hussein. With the Iraqi dictator waging war against Khomeini's Iran, and with the United States secretly funneling weapons to his bogged-down military, by 1988 Hussein was so integral to the Reagan administration's realpolitik policy in the region that it simply looked the other way when Hussein launched the murderous Anfal campaign against his Kurdish subjects. A squalid new low was reached in March of that year, when Iraqi forces poison-gassed the Kurdish town Halabja, killing an estimated 5,000 people. Despite overwhelming evidence that Hussein was responsible for the atrocity — Halabja would figure prominently in his 2006 trial for crimes against humanity — Reagan-administration officials scurried to suggest it was actually the handiwork of Iran.

What finally ended the American arrangement with Saddam Hussein was the Iraqi despot's 1990 decision to invade neighboring Kuwait, upsetting not just the Western powers but also most of his Arab neighbors. Perversely, that event very nearly led to yet another slaughter of Iraq's Kurds. Instead, it would eventually lead to their liberation, as well as mark the crucial moment when the United States propelled itself headlong into Iraq's sectarian and ethnic divides.

In the face of Hussein's belligerence, President George H.W. Bush marshaled an international military coalition — Operation Desert Storm — that swiftly annihilated the Iraqi Army in Kuwait, then rolled into Iraq itself. With Hussein's government appearing on the verge of collapse, Bush encouraged the Iraqi people to rise up in revolt. Both of Iraq's marginalized communities — the Shiites in the south and the Kurds in the north — eagerly did so, only to see the United States suddenly take pause. Belatedly concluding that Hussein's demise might play into the hands of a still-hostile Iran, the Bush administration ordered American troops to stand down as the Iraqi Army regrouped and began a pitiless counterattack.

To forestall a wholesale massacre of the rebels they had encouraged, the United States joined its allies in establishing a protected buffer zone in Kurdistan, as well as no-fly zones in both northern and southern Iraq. That still left Saddam Hussein in Baghdad, of course, and ready to take his revenge at the first opportunity. While the Bush administration concluded there was little it could do to aid the geographically isolated Shiites in the south — they soon suffered their own Anfal-style pogrom — to protect the Kurds, they forced Hussein to militarily withdraw from all of Kurdistan. Taking matters a step further, in July 1992 the Kurdistan Regional Government, an autonomous union of Iraq's three Kurdish provinces, was established.

The Bush administration most likely regarded this Kurdish separation as a stopgap measure, to be undone once the tyrant in Baghdad had gone and the danger had passed. The long-suffering Kurds of Iraq saw it very differently. For the first time since 1919, they were free from the yoke of Baghdad, and they had their own nation in all but name. While very few in the West appreciated the significance at the time, the creation of the Kurdistan Regional Government, or K.R.G., marked the first dismantling of the colonial borders that were imposed on the region 75 years earlier, the de facto partition of one of the Middle East's artificial nations. In the years just ahead, tens of thousands of members of the Iraqi Kurdish diaspora would abandon their places of exile to return to their old homeland. In 1994, that included a 19-year-old college student, Azar Mirkhan, who had spent almost his entire life as a refugee in Iran.

4.

Majd Ibrahim
Syria

BEFORE ITS destruction, Homs was a pleasant-enough place, a city of roughly 800,000 in the flat interior of Syria's central valley, but close enough to the foothills of the coastal mountain range to escape the worst of the region's tremendous summer heat. It was never a spot where tourists tarried very long. Although Homs dated back to before Greek and Roman times, little of the ancient had been preserved, and whatever visitors happened through the town tended to make quickly for Krak des Chevaliers, the famous Crusader castle 30 miles to the west. There was an interesting covered souk in the Old City and a graceful if unremarkable old mosque, but otherwise Homs looked much like any other modern Syrian city. A collection of drab and peeling government buildings dominated downtown, surrounded by neighborhoods of five- and six-story apartment buildings; in its outlying districts could be seen the unadorned cinder-block homes and jutting rebar that give so many Middle Eastern suburbs the look of an ongoing construction site, or a recently abandoned one.

Yet, until its demise, Homs had the distinction of being the most religiously diverse city in one of the most religiously mixed countries in the Arab world. Nationally, Syria is composed of about 70 percent Arab Sunni Muslims, 12 percent Alawites — an offshoot of Shia Islam — and a roughly equal percentage of Sunni Kurds; Christians and a number of smaller religious sects make up the rest. At the geographic crossroads of Syria, Homs reflected this ecumenical confluence, with a skyline punctuated not just by the minarets of mosques but also by the steeples of Catholic churches and the domes of Orthodox Christian ones.

This gave Homs a cosmopolitan flavor not readily found elsewhere — so much so that in 1997, the Ibrahims, a Sunni couple, thought nothing of putting their first child, 5-year-old Majd, in a private Catholic school. As a result, Majd grew up with mostly Christian friends and a better knowledge of Jesus and the Bible than of Muhammad and the Quran. This didn't appear to bother Majd's parents at all. Although raised as Muslims, both were of the nominal variety, with his mother rarely even bothering to wear a head scarf in public and his father dragging himself to the mosque only for funerals.

Such secular liberalism was very much in keeping with the new Syria that Hafez al-Assad sought to shape during his otherwise typically iron-fisted 30-year dictatorship, a secularism undoubtedly encouraged by his own religious minority status as an Alawite. After his death in 2000, the policy was carried on by his son, Bashar. A bland and socially awkward London-trained ophthalmologist, Bashar came to power largely by default — the Assad patriarch had been grooming his eldest son, Bassel, to take over until a fatal car accident in 1994. But Bashar, while projecting a softer, more modern face of Baathism to the outside world, also proved adroit at navigating the tricky currents of Middle Eastern politics. While still publicly vowing to recover the Golan Heights taken by Israel in the Six-Day War, he maintained an uneasy détente with Tel Aviv, even pursuing secret negotiations toward a settlement. By gradually loosening Syria's hold on neighboring Lebanon — its troops had occupied portions of the country since 1976, and Damascus was a prime supporter of Lebanon's Hezbollah militia — the younger Assad was viewed increasingly favorably by the West.

And to a young Majd Ibrahim then coming of age, it increasingly appeared that it was the West where his nation's future lay. Like other middle-class boys in Homs, he wore Western clothes, listened to Western music, watched Western videos, but Majd was also afforded a unique window onto the outside world. His father, an electrical engineer, worked at one of the best hotels in Homs, the Safir, and Majd — fascinated by the hotel, with its constant bustle of travelers — made any excuse to visit him as he went about his day. For Majd, the Safir was also a place of reassurance, a reminder that no matter what small deviations Syrian politics took along the way, he would always be able to inhabit the modern and secular world into which he was born.

PART II: THE IRAQ WAR

2003–2011

5.

Khulood al-Zaidi
Iraq

AS THE SECOND-YOUNGEST of six children — three boys and three girls — born to a hospital radiologist and his stay-at-home wife, Khulood al-Zaidi had a relatively comfortable middle-class childhood. But like most of the other girls in Kut, a low-slung provincial city of some 400,000 located 100 miles down the Tigris River from Baghdad, she lived a life that was both cloistered and highly regimented: off to school each day and then straight home to help with household chores, followed by more study. Save for school, Khulood seldom ventured from home for anything beyond the occasional family outing or to help her mother and older sisters with the grocery shopping. In 23 years, she had left her hometown only once, a day trip to Baghdad chaperoned by her father.

Yet, in the peculiar way that ambition can take root in the most inhospitable of settings, Khulood had always been determined to escape the confines of Kut, and she focused her energies on the one path that might allow for it: higher education. In this, she had an ally of sorts in her father. Ali al-Zaidi was insistent that all his children, including his three daughters, obtain college degrees, even if the ultimate purpose of the girls' education bordered on the obscure.

"My father was very progressive in a lot of ways," she explained, "but even with him, going to college was never about my having a professional career. Instead, it was always the idea of 'Study hard, get a degree, but then find a husband.'" She shrugged. "This was the Iraqi system." Khulood pursued a degree in English literature at a local university, but the expectation was that, degree in hand, she might teach English at a local school for a few years, then marry and start a family. Khulood had different plans, though: With her English proficiency, she would go to Baghdad and look for work as an interpreter for one of the few foreign companies then operating in Iraq.

That scheme was sidetracked when, just three months short of her graduation, the Americans invaded Iraq. In the early morning of April 3, 2003, the fighting reached Kut. Advance units of the United States First Marine Expeditionary Force encircled the city, and for the next several hours methodically destroyed one Iraqi redoubt after another, their tanks and artillery on the ground complemented by close air support. Of this battle for her hometown, Khulood, then 23, heard a great deal but saw nothing. There was a simple explanation for this. "Women weren't allowed out of the house," she said.

Before the invasion, Vice President Dick Cheney predicted that Americans would be "greeted as liberators" in Iraq, and his prediction was borne out in the streets of Kut on April 4. As the Marines consolidated their hold on the city, they were happily swarmed by young men and children proffering trays of sweets and hot tea. Finally permitted to leave her home, Khulood, like most other women in Kut, observed the spectacle from a discreet distance. "The Americans were very relaxed, friendly, but mostly I was struck by how huge they seemed — and all their weapons and vehicles, too. Everything seemed out of scale, like we had been invaded by aliens."

While there continued to be sporadic fighting elsewhere by remnants of Saddam Hussein's Baathist government — given the Orwellian label of "anti-Iraqi forces" by the Bush administration — the few coalition troops who remained in Kut that spring and early summer felt secure enough to mingle free of body armor with residents and to patrol its streets in unprotected trucks. Those soldiers also quickly returned the city to something close to normalcy. The university was reopened after just a two-month interruption, enabling Khulood to obtain her bachelor's degree that August. The real work now was in rebuilding the nation's shattered economy and reconstituting its government, and to that end a small army of foreign engineers, accountants and consultants descended on Iraq under the aegis of the Coalition Provisional Authority, or C.P.A., the American-led transitional administration that would stand down once a new Iraqi government was in place.

One of those who came was a 33-year-old lawyer from Oklahoma named Fern Holland. A human rights adviser for the C.P.A., Holland had a special brief in the summer of 2003 that included developing projects to empower women in the Shiite heartland of southern Iraq. In September 2003, that mission took her to Kut and her first encounter with Khulood.

"I will always remember the first time I saw Fern," Khulood said. "She brought a group of us women together to talk about the work she wanted to do in Iraq. She was surprisingly young — this is easy to forget, because her personality was so strong — with bright blond hair and a very open, friendly manner. I had never met a woman like her. I don't think any of us in that room had."

What Holland told the women in the Kut meeting hall was no less exotic to them than her appearance. With the overthrow of Saddam Hussein, she said, a new Iraq was being established, one in which democracy and respect for human rights would reign supreme. What's more, to consolidate this new Iraq, everyone had a role to play, not least the women of Kut.

For Khulood, that talk struck with the force of epiphany. This was the moment she had been waiting for her entire life. Almost immediately, she began doing volunteer work on women's rights projects for Holland. "I had thought about these issues before, but under Saddam Hussein they were like fantasies," Khulood said. "Now, I saw a future for myself."

Holland was perhaps less confident. From past experience working in conservative and male-dominated societies in Africa, she suspected that it would only be a matter of time — and probably a very short time — before the forces of tradition rose up in opposition to her work, so she had to set change in motion quickly. She also knew that, as an outsider, her role needed to be a limited one; what was required was dynamic local women to spearhead the effort, women like Khulood al-Zaidi.

The following month, Holland chose Khulood to be a representative at a national women's leadership conference, held under the auspices of the C.P.A. At that conference, Khulood received even headier news: She had been selected as part of a women's delegation that would soon travel to Washington to help draft the new Iraqi Constitution. When word of this spread at the conference, it provoked a backlash. "A lot of the other women objected because I was so young," Khulood said. "Even I thought it was maybe too much. But Fern insisted. She told the other women, 'Khulood represents the youth of Iraq — she is going.' She was my biggest supporter."

On that November 2003 trip to Washington, the 23-year-old fresh out of college met with a parade of dignitaries, including President George W. Bush. Upon her return, she was formally hired by the C.P.A. to serve as an assistant manager of the Kut media office. It was a very long way for a young woman who, less than a year earlier, had imagined no greater future than finding interpreter work with a foreign company. "It was a very exciting time," Khulood said. "Because you could feel everything changing so fast."

6.

Wakaz Hassan
Iraq

WAKAZ HASSAN IS saved from ordinariness by his eyes. In most every other way, the tall and gangly 22-year-old would appear unremarkable, just one more face in the crowd — but so intensely dark and arresting are his eyes that you might initially think he was wearing mascara. In his stare is a kind of mournful impenetrability that hints at the hard world he has seen.

Only 8 years old in 2003, Wakaz seemed destined for an exceedingly normal life, even a prosaic one. The youngest of five children born to an Iraqi bank clerk and his wife, he spent his childhood in the drowsy farming community of Dawr, just 15 miles down the Tigris River from Saddam

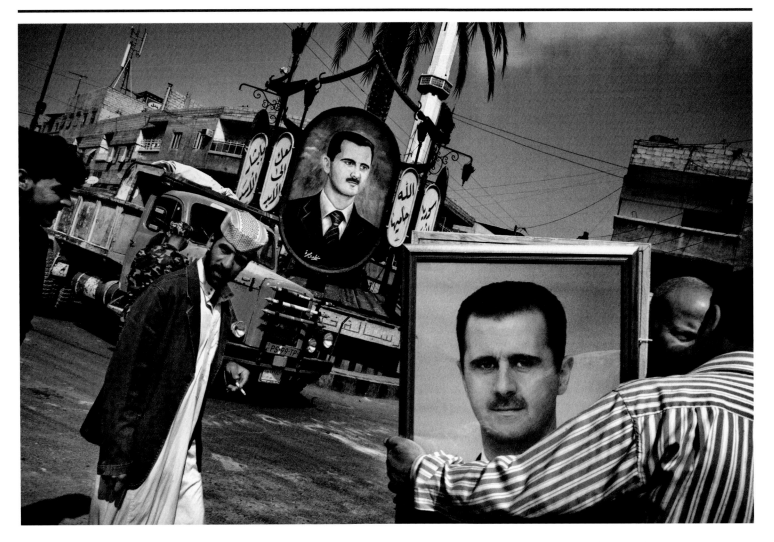

Hussein's hometown, Tikrit. "All was very good there," he recalled. "Easy."

That changed with the American invasion. Long considered a Baathist stronghold by virtue of Hussein's origins there, Tikrit and its environs were a prime early objective of the invaders, with the city itself the target of intense aerial bombardments. By mid-April 2003, coalition troops occupied the string of gaudy palace buildings erected by Hussein along the Tikrit riverfront and began conducting raids through the surrounding river towns in search of fugitive Baathist officials. The May 15 raid on Dawr netted 30 suspected Baathists — a startling number for such a small community — but the town was soon to yield up an even greater prize. In mid-December 2003, American troops discovered a "spider hole" on the northern edge of Dawr and pulled out Hussein himself.

The young Wakaz had only the vaguest grasp of all this. According to him, his family — Sunni, like most all residents of the Tikrit area — was not particularly religious, nor was it political in any way. He remembered hearing something about the mistreatment of Iraqi prisoners at an American-operated prison — clearly a reference to the Abu Ghraib scandal — and then there was the time

American soldiers searched his family's home, but those soldiers were quite respectful, and the episode passed without incident.

"I know others had problems with the Americans," Wakaz said, "but my family, no. For us, we were really not affected at all."

What the Hassan family did blame the invaders for, at least in a general way, was the ensuing collapse of the Iraqi economy, a downturn that cost Wakaz's father his job at the Rafidain Bank. To support his young family, the Hassan patriarch used his savings to open a small sweet shop on Dawr's main street. "So yes, our life was definitely much easier before the Americans came," Wakaz conceded. "Even if it wasn't their fault directly, that is when everything became much harder."

7.

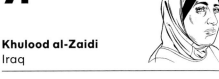

Khulood al-Zaidi
Iraq

AS SHE ENTERED the new world opened up to her by Fern Holland, Khulood remained unaware

that the seeds of disaster for the American intervention had already been sown.

In their Iraqi war plans, the Pentagon had set down comprehensive blueprints detailing which strategic installations and government ministries were to be seized and guarded. But the American military seemed to have given little thought to the arsenals and munitions depots that Hussein had scattered about the country. In one town and city after another, these storehouses were systematically looted, sometimes under the gaze of coalition soldiers who did not intervene.

The occupying authorities soon compounded this misstep. In a move now largely regarded as calamitous, one of the first actions taken by the C.P.A.'s administrator, Paul Bremer, was to disband the Iraqi military. Just like that, hundreds of thousands of men — men with both military training and access to weapons — were being put out of their jobs by the summer of 2003.

It may have been the edict immediately preceding that decree, however, that had the most deleterious effect. Under the terms of C.P.A. Order No. 1, senior Baath Party members were summarily dismissed from government positions and placed under a lifetime public-employment ban. In addition, employees in the upper echelon of all government institutions were to be investigated for Baathist affiliations. As critics pointed out, tens of thousands of apolitical Iraqi professionals — a group that included Khulood's radiologist father, Ali al-Zaidi — were compelled to join the party in the 1990s as part of a "recruitment drive" by Saddam Hussein; now these teachers and doctors and engineers were at risk of being disenfranchised.

The effects of Order 1 stretched far beyond the dismissed Baathists. In Iraq, as in much of the rest of the Middle East, government offices operated on an elaborate patronage system in which most every employee, from senior staff down to the steward who brought refreshments to visitors, owed their jobs to the head man; as might be expected, that man — almost invariably a Baath Party member during Saddam Hussein's reign — usually handed out those jobs to members of his extended family or tribe. What the firing of as many as 85,000 Baathists actually meant, then, was the cashiering of countless more people and the instant impoverishment of entire clans and tribes.

Under the weight of these blunders, it's remarkable that the Iraqi occupation didn't blow up sooner. An omen of what was to come occurred in August 2003, when the United Nations headquarters in Baghdad was destroyed by a truck bomb, killing 22, including the U.N.'s special representative for Iraq, Sergio Vieira de Mello. That was followed by a steady escalation in attacks against coalition forces. By the beginning of 2004, C.P.A. officials perceived a deepening hostility toward their initiatives, so much so that even Fern Holland began to worry. As she wrote in an email to a friend in late January: "We're doing all we can with the brief time we've got left. It's a terrible race. Wish us luck. Wish the Iraqis luck."

On March 8, 2004, the new provisional Constitution of Iraq was signed. The clause that set a goal of having 25 percent of future parliamentary seats held by women was largely credited to the behind-the-scenes lobbying of Fern Holland.

The following afternoon, a Daewoo containing three C.P.A. civilian employees was traveling along a provincial highway when an Iraqi police pickup truck pulled alongside. With a blast of automatic gunfire, the car was sent careering across the highway before stalling on the shoulder; the men in the police truck then clambered out to finish off their victims with assault rifles. All three of the Daewoo's occupants were killed in the fusillade, marking them as the first C.P.A. civilians to be murdered in Iraq. That included the driver and presumed target of the attack, Fern Holland.

Following Holland's murder, a sense of trepidation spread among the thousands of C.P.A.

personnel scattered across Iraq. "We were all in a state of shock, of course," Khulood al-Zaidi said, "but I think we were also waiting to see what it meant, if it had been an attack on Fern in particular or if this was going to be something larger."

The answer came very soon. In tandem with the growing Sunni insurgency in central Iraq, through the first months of 2004, a radical Shiite cleric in Baghdad, Moktada al-Sadr, had been demanding a withdrawal of all coalition forces from the nation. In early April, Sadr unleashed his militia, the Mahdi Army, in an effort to bring that withdrawal about through a series of well-coordinated attacks against military and C.P.A. installations. Kut's turn came on April 5, when some 200 Mahdi militiamen began attacking the C.P.A. compound.

Khulood spent hours trapped in the C.P.A. media office, as the coalition forces assigned to guard the compound returned fire. Finally a C.P.A. supervisor turned to Khulood. "If you are not afraid," he said, "you should just go."

With two other local workers, Khulood managed to thread her way out of the compound and, dodging down side alleys, to escape. With the C.P.A. compound subsequently abandoned, she remained in hiding as the Mahdi militiamen who now controlled Kut searched for any local C.P.A. employees left behind. Even after American forces retook the city, Khulood remained so frightened she didn't leave her family's home for two weeks.

The Mahdi uprising radically altered the flow of events in Iraq. Both Sunni and Shia militias sharply increased their attacks against coalition forces, marking the true beginning of the Iraq war. Despite this, the C.P.A. went ahead with their program of ceding control of Iraq to a new central government. In May, the last of the foreign civilians based in Kut began withdrawing, and within two months, the whole of the local C.P.A. infrastructure was placed under the authority of the new Baghdad government.

For a time, this did seem to calm passions in Khulood's hometown, enough so that she vowed to continue the women's rights initiatives begun by her murdered mentor. That autumn, she helped found a small nongovernmental organization called Al-Batul, or Virgin. Its goals were modest. "Kut has a small Christian population," Khulood explained, "so my idea was to bring Christian and Muslim women together to work on projects that were important to both communities. It was mainly to teach the women how to defend their rights, to show them that they didn't always have to obey what men said."

But in the deepening sectarianism spreading across Iraq, Sunni and Shia militants alike increasingly viewed the Christian community as the infidels within; in turn, terrified Christians were beginning to abandon the nation in droves,

an exodus that would eventually reduce their numbers in Iraq by more than two-thirds. Further, the only possible source of funding for an endeavor like Al-Batul was from the foreign occupiers, enabling militants to denounce it as a front in the service of the enemy. Almost immediately, Khulood began receiving anonymous threats for continuing her work on "American issues," threats that escalated to the point where she was denounced by name in a local newspaper.

The memory of that time caused Khulood, now 36, to become somber, reflective. "I can see now that I was quite naïve, that I didn't take the situation as seriously as I should have. But my feeling was that I was only working on things that might give women a better life, so how was I a threat?"

In October 2004, the Al-Batul office in Kut was shot up. Undeterred, Khulood rented a second office, only to have it looted. That January, while attending a human rights training seminar in Amman, the capital of neighboring Jordan, she received a warning: If she resumed her work in Kut, she would be killed. She remained in Jordan for three months, but in April 2005 — a year after the death of Fern Holland and with the fighting in Iraq now spiraling into sectarian war — Khulood finally slipped back to her hometown.

She recognizes now that this decision bordered on the foolhardy. "It was just very difficult for me to give up on this dream I had for Iraq," Khulood said, recalling how Holland told her that "to bring change it takes people with courage, that sometimes you have to push very hard. Well, I didn't want to die, but Fern had, and I think I held onto this hope that if we kept trying, maybe things would improve."

Shortly after returning to Kut, Khulood went to the local police station to file a report about her looted office, only to be treated dismissively. A more ominous note was struck when she met with one of her old Al-Batul colleagues. "Why did you come back here?" the woman asked. "Everyone knows you're working for the American Embassy." Her colleague's accusation came on the heels of a call summoning Khulood to the local militia headquarters. "That's when I finally saw there was no chance for me in Iraq, that if I tried any longer, they would surely kill me."

8.

Laila Soueif
Egypt

AS KHULOOD WAS planning her escape from Iraq in April 2005, Laila Soueif was escalating her opposition to the Egyptian dictatorship of Hosni Mubarak.

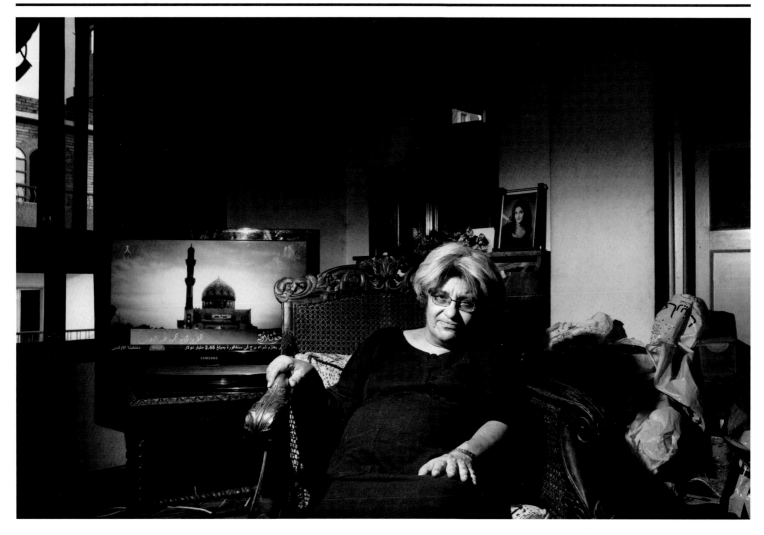

By then, Laila and her husband, Ahmed Seif, had been Egypt's most celebrated political dissident couple for well over a decade, serving as constant nuisances to the Mubarak government. Since his release from prison in 1989, Ahmed had become the nation's pre-eminent human rights lawyer, the champion of an eclectic array of defendants in politically motivated cases that included leftist university professors, Islamic fundamentalists and — in a nation where homosexuality remains effectively illegal — members of Cairo's gay community. When I first met him that autumn, Ahmed was involved in perhaps the most controversial case of his career, defending a group of men accused of complicity in a 2004 hotel bombing in the Sinai Peninsula that left 31 dead.

For her part, and even while retaining her mathematics professorship at Cairo University, Laila had gained a reputation as one of Cairo's most indefatigable "street" leaders, the veteran of countless protest marches against the government. Part of what drove her was a keen awareness that, as a member of the Cairene professional class, she enjoyed a freedom to dissent that was all but denied to Egypt's poor

and working class. "Historically," she said, "that bestowed a degree of immunity — the security forces really didn't like to mess with us, because they didn't know who in the power structure we could call up — but that also meant we had a responsibility, to be a voice for those who are silenced. And being a woman helped, too. In this culture, women just aren't taken that seriously, so it allows you to do things that men can't."

But she was also quite aware that her activism — and the government's grudging tolerance of it — fit neatly into the divide-and-rule strategy that Hosni Mubarak had employed since assuming power in 1981. In the past, Egyptian governments were able to gin up bipartisan support when needed by playing the anti-West, anti-Israel card, but Anwar Sadat traded that card away by making peace with Israel and going on the American payroll. The new strategy consisted of allowing an expanded level of political dissent among the small, urban educated class, while swiftly moving to crush any sign of growing influence by the far more numerous — and therefore, far more dangerous — Islamists.

In Laila's estimation, what finally caused this strategy to fray was the launch of the second

Palestinian intifada, or uprising, against Israel in September 2000. With most Egyptians of all political persuasions holding that their government sold out the Palestinians with the 1979 peace treaty with Israel, Mubarak was suddenly powerless to muzzle pro-Palestinian demonstrations lest he be seen as an even greater lackey of the Americans. "For the first time," Laila explained, "we began organizing openly and publicly without taking any permission from the government and without taking cover under any of the so-called legitimate political parties. And what was the government going to do about it? This established the pattern — you don't wait for permission, you don't look for an existing political party to take you in, you just organize — that we used many, many times afterward."

In short order, street protests became a constant feature of Egyptian life. Even more deleterious from the government's point of view, fury over the Palestinian situation galvanized opposition groups from across the political spectrum to march and work together.

With this new dynamic in place, the last thing Hosni Mubarak needed was another reminder to the Egyptian people of his fealty to Washington

— but then came the United States' decision to invade Iraq.

While astute enough to oppose that invasion in public, and to engage in high-profile diplomacy to try to head it off, Mubarak wasn't able to escape its fallout. In the eyes of many Egyptians, after 23 years of taking lucre from the Americans, the dictator was simply too much their puppet to make a show of independence now. That cynical view only hardened as the war in Iraq dragged on and the daily body count mounted. From 2002 through early 2005, some of the largest antiwar demonstrations in the Arab world were taking place in the streets of Cairo, and Laila Soueif was on the front lines in nearly every one of them. "Of course, on the overt level it was to protest what was occurring in Iraq," Laila said, "but this also reflected the failure of Mubarak."

At the same time, the dictator did himself few favors with a series of domestic initiatives that further inflamed the opposition. Grooming his son Gamal as his successor, in February 2005 Mubarak engineered a rewriting of the Constitution that, while ostensibly allowing for direct presidential elections, actually rigged the system so as to make domination by his political party all but perpetual. In presidential elections that September, Mubarak won a fifth six-year term with nearly 89 percent of the vote, after having arrested the only notable candidate to stand against him, Ayman Nour. Under mounting pressure at home and abroad, he reduced his interference in the November 2005 parliamentary elections, only to see the Muslim Brotherhood, an Islamist party still officially banned, take an unprecedented 20 percent of the seats.

By late 2005, when I spent six weeks traveling through Egypt, growing contempt for the government was evident everywhere. To be sure, much of that antipathy derived from the nation's economic stagnation and from the corruption that had enabled a small handful of politicians and generals to become fabulously rich — the Mubarak family financial portfolio alone was reported to run into the billions — but it also had a strong anti-American component, and pointed up a profound disjuncture. At the same time that Egypt was regarded in Washington as one of the United States' most reliable allies in the Arab world, in no small part because of its continuing entente with Israel, over the course of scores of interviews with Egyptians of most every political and religious persuasion, I failed to meet a single one who supported the Israeli peace settlement, or who regarded the American subsidies to the Mubarak government, then approaching $2 billion a year, as anything other than a source of national shame. As Essam el-Erian, deputy head of the Muslim Brotherhood, bluntly told me: "The only politics in Egypt now are the politics of the street, and for anyone to

work with the Americans is to write their political death sentence."

It was during this time of ferment that the three children of Laila Soueif and Ahmed Seif, who previously had shown little interest in activism, began to have a change of heart about politics. The first to make the evolution was their son, Alaa, a pioneering Egyptian blogger, and it happened when he accompanied Laila to a protest march in May 2005.

"He had become very interested in citizen journalism," Laila said, "so with all the street actions surrounding the Constitution and Mubarak running again, he had begun coming down to cover the demonstrations — not to participate, just to report on them."

But the protest on May 25 was a very different affair. Waiting in ambush were government-hired thugs, or *baltageya,* who immediately charged at the demonstrators to beat them with fists and wooden staffs. Perhaps recognizing the well-known protester in their midst, the goons soon fell on Laila.

"Well, this was something new," she said, "for them to punch a middle-aged woman, and when my son saw that, he jumped in to help me." For his trouble, Alaa was beaten up as well. "He had some toes broken, so we went to hospital, and it was only later that we discovered we were the lucky ones. After we left, the *baltageya* began pulling the clothes off women and beating them in their underwear. This was something they did a lot later on, to humiliate, but that was when it began and when Alaa joined the protests. The girls became involved later — Mona got pulled in with the judges' independence movement, and then for Sanaa it was the revolution — but for Alaa, it started in 2005."

Laila Soueif is a tough, unsentimental woman, and if she harbored any pride — or, in light of what was to come, regret — over her children's turn to activism, she didn't let on. "I never tried to dissuade them. Even if I had wanted to — and I probably did at times — I didn't. That kind of thing is useless. They're not going to listen to you anyway, so you just get into fights."

9.

Majdi el-Mangoush
Libya

IT WAS AROUND this time that Majdi el-Mangoush joined onlookers on a sidewalk in his hometown, Misurata, to witness an incredible sight.

Along Tripoli Street, one of the city's main thoroughfares, a municipal work crew with a cherry-picker was methodically taking down the posters of Muammar el-Qaddafi that hung from every lamppost.

It was part of an attempt by the Libyan dictator to put a kinder, gentler face on his government. While ostensibly directed at the Libyan people, the campaign was really meant for Western consumption.

In the days leading up to the invasion of Iraq, there had been talk in President George W. Bush's inner circle that once Saddam Hussein was dispensed with, the troublesome Qaddafi would be next. Once the Iraq invasion began in March 2003, the Libyan dictator hurried to make amends with the Americans. He offered a settlement over his country's role in the 1988 bombing of Pan Am Flight 103 over Lockerbie, Scotland — without explicitly admitting guilt, the Libyan government agreed to set aside $2.7 billion in compensation to the families of the 270 victims — and began quietly dismantling his nation's fledgling program for chemical, biological and nuclear weapons. Even more quietly, Libyan intelligence agents shared dossiers with their American counterparts on suspected Al Qaeda operatives and other Islamic fundamentalists in the region. On the home front, the goal was to create at least the illusion of political liberalization, and one aspect was to remove some of the tens of thousands of posters and billboards of "the Leader" that wallpapered the nation.

Qaddafi soon thought better of the whole egalitarian makeover. By 2006, the United States had restored full diplomatic relations with his government; while officially a response to the abandonment of the Libyan unconventional-weapons program, certainly a contributing factor was that, amid the deepening quagmire of the Iraqi misadventure, there was not going to be any grand American crusade against the region's other dictators. Which also meant that Qaddafi could quietly abandon his reform drive. "It was just a bit of theater," Majdi said. "Nothing really changed, and after a few months, I don't think anyone even remembered it."

But that day hadn't yet arrived when the cherry-picker made its way down Misurata's Tripoli Street. Majdi was still observing the spectacle when an elderly man emerged from a nearby alley.

For a long moment, the old man stared slack-jawed in amazement at the sight before him. He then rushed over to one of the discarded posters, removed a shoe and — in a gesture of insult common throughout the Arab world — began beating it against Qaddafi's likeness amid a torrent of curses.

A municipal worker came over to ask what he was doing.

"The bastard's gone at last, no?" the old man asked. "There's been a coup?"

When the worker set him straight, the man stammered out an explanation for his behavior — he'd been very ill lately, given to fits of lunacy — and then hurried away.

10.

Khulood al-Zaidi
Jordan • United States
• Iraq

KHULOOD DID NOT flee Iraq alone. She crossed back into Jordan with her next-eldest sister, Sahar, and they were joined in Amman a few months later by their father and oldest sister, Teamim. Choosing to stay on in Iraq were Khulood's three brothers, along with her mother, Aziza. By summer 2007, Khulood was especially worried about Wisam, her youngest brother. "The war then was at its worst," she said, "and young men were just being taken from the streets. I called Wisam all the time. I told him there was no future for him in Iraq, that he had to come out, but he was very softhearted and said that he needed to stay to take care of our mother."

One evening that September, as Wisam and a friend walked along a Kut street, someone with an assault rifle killed them both in a burst of gunfire. "He was 25," Khulood said softly. "Some

people say he was killed because of the work I was doing, but I hope that isn't true."

A few months after Wisam's murder, Khulood faced a new ordeal when, working for an NGO, she rebuffed the demands of a corrupt but well-placed Jordanian businessman looking for kickbacks. He was the wrong person to cross. Shortly after, she was ordered to leave Jordan. Facing almost-certain death if forced to return to Iraq, Khulood turned to the United Nations High Commissioner for Refugees for emergency resettlement in a third country.

Among the more unlikely possibilities for resettlement was the United States. In 2008, American troops were still embroiled in an Iraqi civil war, and the Bush administration had strict caps in place (albeit recently loosened) on the number of Iraqis to be given refuge; to let in all those who had fled the country — and there were an estimated half-million displaced Iraqis in Jordan alone — would belie its talking point that the corner had finally been turned in the war. In light of the grave danger Khulood faced, however, the U.N.H.C.R. placed her in its own special program, reserved for only the most vulnerable of refugees, and for those in

this pool, the Americans had a spot available. In July 2008, Khulood boarded a plane bound for San Francisco.

It's hard to imagine a more extreme transition, from the cramped, tumbledown apartment she shared with her father and two sisters in Amman to a pleasant one-bedroom in San Francisco, and Khulood reveled in her new life. "Just to have the freedom to go wherever I wanted, and to not think something bad might happen to me. And I don't mean just the war. For a woman to travel alone in Iraq — maybe it happened in Baghdad, but never in Kut, and so some days I would just take a bus or the metro for hours. It was something I had never really imagined before."

Her career prospects were also much improved. In Iraq, Khulood studied English because it seemed to offer the greatest chance at future freedom for a young woman, but in the United States the opportunities were endless. "After one year, I would get my green card, and then I could apply for scholarships to study whatever I wanted. I became very ambitious."

The one continuing source of worry was for her divided family back in Iraq and Jordan.

While she knew those in Kut wouldn't leave, Khulood was desperate to release her father and sisters from their limbo existence in Amman and, soon after reaching San Francisco, she started the paperwork to have them join her.

Three months later, Khulood received both good and bad news. Her two sisters were approved for resettlement. Their father, however, was rejected. The sisters remained in Jordan while the family appealed the decision, but Ali al-Zaidi was rejected again.

By February 2009, seven months after Khulood's arrival in San Francisco, there was still no progress in the effort to resettle her father. It was then she made a fateful decision: She would return to Jordan and work on his case there.

"My friends in San Francisco couldn't understand it," she recalled. "Why, when you have a new life here, why would you ever go back?" Khulood grew thoughtful for a moment, as if still struggling for an answer. "But how to explain my culture to them? In Iraq, family is the most important thing, you can never turn away from it, so how could I and my sisters enjoy this nice life in America but leave our father behind? We could never live with the shame of that. So I went back."

In Amman, Khulood tirelessly pursued any angle she could think of to win her father's exit, petitioning for settlement not just in the United States but also in a half-dozen European nations. Nothing worked.

Worse, Khulood had walked herself into legal limbo. As she was warned before leaving San Francisco, under the stipulations of American immigration law, refugees awaiting the permanent status of a green card cannot leave the country for longer than six months. By returning — and staying — in Jordan, Khulood had lost her refugee classification. Now, along with the part

of her family that she had brought out of Iraq, Khulood was stranded. She could not go home or to a third country, hostage to the whim of a state — Jordan — that was anxious to shed her.

11.

Majd Ibrahim
Syria

THE AMERICAN INVASION of Iraq was initially worrisome for Bashar al-Assad. The Syrian dictator's relations with the mercurial and dangerous Saddam Hussein had warmed recently, and he was no doubt concerned that he could be next on the American hit list. But just as with Muammar el-Qaddafi in Libya, by the late 2000s, Assad could be quite confident that he had nothing to fear from a flailing United States.

Not that this confidence translated into greater political freedom for the Syrian people. Just as in his father's day, Assad's subjects lived in constant fear of internal security agents and a network of government-sanctioned thugs, or *shabiha*. So pervasive was this spying apparatus — or at least the fear of it — that politics wasn't so much a delicate subject in most Syrian homes as no subject at all.

"I can never remember my father saying anything about the regime, good or bad," Majd Ibrahim said. "And I never remember any of my relatives or neighbors doing it either. When it came to the state, the most anyone would criticize was maybe the corrupt traffic policeman at the corner. You just didn't talk about that stuff with anyone."

Because of his liberal upbringing, Majd experienced a shock when he left his Catholic school at the end of the ninth grade and transferred

into a state high school. His modern and secular ways often estranged him from his more Islamist-minded classmates, and the instruction was abysmal. But high school is a bad time for a lot of people, and Majd's life brightened considerably upon graduating in summer 2010. While failing to obtain the high marks on the national exam that would have enabled him to pursue one of the "higher" professions — engineering or medicine — he did sufficiently well to enter Al-Baath University in Homs that autumn to pursue a degree in hotel management.

This was undoubtedly a better fit for Majd regardless. The handsome, outgoing young man had a natural charm that enabled him to develop a quick rapport with most anyone, joined to an intense curiosity about the larger world beyond Homs. With his degree in hand, he envisioned a future at one of the luxury hotels in Damascus — they "represented one of the best ways to advance," he said, "to have a good life."

But there was another feature of his hometown that Majd had probably scarcely given thought to in his short life: In almost every way, Homs truly was the crossroads of Syria. Located near the midpoint of the highway between the nation's two largest cities, Damascus and Aleppo, Homs was also the eastern terminus of the highway linking Syria's interior to its coastal provinces. Just as significant, it was the hub of the nation's gas- and oil-refinery industry — quite logically, since the pipelines leading from the oil and natural-gas fields in the eastern deserts passed directly through the city on their way to the coast. If all this served to make Homs a prosperous town, it also meant that, in the event of a war, it was a place all sides would fight furiously to control.

By the time Majd started at Al-Baath University, that war was just months away.

PART III: ARAB SPRING

2011–2014

12.

Laila Soueif
Egypt

LAILA HAD BEEN involved with Egyptian politics for far too long to believe all the talk about the plans to protest in Tahrir Square on Jan. 25, 2011. "It's not going to be a demonstration," one young activist told her. "It's going to be a revolution." She understood the man's excitement. Only days earlier, street protests after the self-immolation of the fruit-and-vegetable vendor in Tunisia had forced the longtime Tunisian strongman Zine el-Abidine Ben Ali from power. Throughout the Arab world, rebellion was in the air. But this was Egypt. Laila expected news conferences and solidarity committee meetings, perhaps some paper reforms, certainly not insurrection. She even joked about it. She was attending an educational conference the day before the demonstration, and when an organizer asked if she would be returning the next day, she replied, "Well, tomorrow we're having a revolution, but if the revolution ends early, yes, I'll be here."

The following day, as Laila approached Tahrir Square, she realized this indeed was something altogether different from the toothless Egyptian protests of the past. Until now, the Cairene activist community had considered a protest successful if it drew several hundred demonstrators. In Tahrir Square on Jan. 25, the crowd was at least 15,000, and Laila soon heard about the many thousands more who had converged on different rallying points around Cairo and in other towns and cities across Egypt. In Tahrir, as elsewhere around the nation, the stunned security forces simply stepped aside, as the emboldened crowds' calls for reform gave way to open demands for Hosni Mubarak's fall.

The protests continued over the next two days, until, on Jan. 28, Laila concluded that they truly did have a revolution on their hands. That morning, she and some friends traveled to the Imbaba neighborhood in northwest Cairo to join a group intending to march on Tahrir, only to be met by a wall of soldiers in riot gear. After dispersing the protesters, the soldiers pursued them into Imbaba's narrow alleyways, firing tear gas as they went.

"That was a very stupid mistake," Laila explained. "These are small alleys where people are practically living in the street, so that just brought down Imbaba. It became a fixed battle between the troops and the residents, and there was absolutely no moving those people. They were going to break down these soldiers and torch the police stations, or die trying."

The battle for Imbaba continued late into the afternoon. Laila, having become separated from her friends, decided to walk to downtown alone. It was an eerie journey. The streets were deserted, and fires raged in the growing dusk: cars, barricades, police stations burning. Echoing off the surrounding buildings came the sound of gunfire, some single shots, others the sustained bursts of assault rifles. With darkness falling, Laila finally emerged onto Ramses Street, a major thoroughfare in central Cairo.

"And suddenly, this huge crowd of demonstrators appeared," she recalled, "running down Ramses. They had just broken through the police cordons, and they were running to get to Tahrir. One young man saw me standing there, and he came over and hugged me — he'd obviously seen me before, in Tahrir — and said, 'I told you we would have a revolution!' And that was the moment when I knew it was true, and that we would be victorious."

Over the next week, both the size and the militancy of the demonstrations grew, but so did the harshness of the government's response, with soldiers and the police increasingly trading tear gas for live ammunition. On Feb. 1, a defiant Mubarak took to the airwaves vowing never to leave Egypt — "On its soil I will die" — and the following day there came the bizarre spectacle, called the Battle of the Camel, when scores of state-sponsored thugs astride horses and camels attacked those encamped in Tahrir Square with riding crops and whips.

The following day, Ahmed Seif's law center was raided by the military police, and he and dozens of others were hauled off for questioning at the headquarters of military intelligence. For two days, Ahmed was interrogated by a variety of officers, but he would have reason to recall one encounter in particular. It came on the morning of Feb. 5, when the chief of military intelligence, a colorless general named Abdel Fattah el-Sisi, going about other business, happened to stride past Ahmed and several other prisoners. In an impromptu lecture, Sisi warned his captive audience that they should all respect Mubarak and Egypt's military leadership and that, once released, they should go home and forget Tahrir Square. When Ahmed, forgoing respectful silence, retorted that Mubarak was corrupt, the general's haughty manner swiftly changed. "He became angry; his face became red," Ahmed recalled a few years later to The Guardian. "He acted as if every citizen would accept his point and no one would reject it in public. When he was rejected in public, he lost it."

Upon his release that day, Ahmed stopped by his home for a change of clothes and then immediately returned to Tahrir Square.

It soon became clear that the regime was losing control. Across Egypt came reports of army units refusing orders to fire on demonstrators, and in Tahrir Square television cameras captured images of soldiers embracing the protesters and sharing cigarettes with them.

On Feb. 11, the clock finally ran out on Hosni Mubarak. After submitting his resignation, the president and his immediate family boarded a plane and fled to their palatial retreat in the Red Sea resort town Sharm el Sheikh. At the news, all of Egypt erupted in celebration, and nowhere more so than in Cairo's Tahrir Square.

But among a small handful of Egyptians, joy was already tinged with a note of disquiet, especially when it was announced that a group of senior military officers, the Supreme Council of the Armed Forces, or SCAF, would serve as an interim government until elections were held. One of those who worried was Laila Soueif.

"In the last few days of Mubarak," she said, "when we could see what was coming, I and some of the other independents, we tried to talk to all the different political factions. 'Seize power. Don't wait for permission. Just seize power now before the military steps in.' And everyone said: 'Yes, of course, that's a good idea. We'll organize a meeting to talk about it in a couple of days.'" Laila shook her head, gave a bitter little laugh. "But maybe it was asking too much. Maybe we simply couldn't do it at that point. People needed to feel they had won. Not us, the politicos, but all these millions of people who had come down to the street. They needed a time to feel victorious." She sighed, and then fell silent for a moment. "I don't know. To this day, I don't know. But I think that was our critical moment, and we lost."

13.

Majdi el-Mangoush
Libya

BY JANUARY 2011, Majdi was completing his third and final year in the national air force academy, a sprawling compound in southwest Misurata, hoping to earn a degree in communications engineering. He was an unlikely soldier — softhearted, slightly pudgy — but the academy was an easy choice for Majdi, allowing him to spend regular leaves at his family home, just a few miles away, and hang out with his civilian friends. He and his fellow cadets followed the news of the upheavals in Tunisia and Egypt in astonishment, but none connected that tumult to their situation in Libya, much less imagined it might spread there. Then, on the evening of Feb. 19, a Saturday, the cadets heard a series of crackling sounds coming from within the city. At first, they thought it might be firecrackers, but the sounds intensified and drew nearer, until the students realized it was gunfire. Soon they were ordered to assemble at the drill ground, where they were informed that all leave had been canceled. By then, the watchtowers that ringed the compound — usually empty or occupied by a single bored sentry — were manned by squads of soldiers with mounted machine guns.

"That's when we knew something big had happened," Majdi recalled, "because this was unlike anything we'd seen before. But still, no one would tell us what was going on."

Majdi hoped he would get an explanation when classes resumed the next morning, but the civilian instructors failed to show up. Throughout that day, Majdi stayed in the constant company of his best friend at the academy, Jalal al-Drisi, a 23-year-old cadet from Benghazi. In contrast to the shy Majdi, Jalal, wiry and quick on his feet, was always ready with an irreverent joke or an elaborate prank. What the two shared was a fascination with science and gadgetry — Jalal was studying aviation weaponry — and over the course of the previous two and a half years, they had become inseparable. Jalal frequently spent his weekend leaves at the Mangoush family home in Misurata, a hospitality that was reciprocated when Majdi spent part of the summer of 2009 with the Drisis in Benghazi. In the bizarre

news-free environment that existed at the academy, the young men tried to puzzle out what was happening.

Over the next two days, the gunfire beyond the walls continued sporadically. The sound would draw near at times, only to recede; intense exchanges would be followed by long periods of quiet.

A measure of clarity finally came on Feb. 22, when Col. Muammar el-Qaddafi, clad in an olive-drab robe, addressed the nation. In what almost instantly became known as the *Zenga Zenga* speech, the dictator laid blame for the social unrest then spreading across Libya on foreign conspirators and "rats," and he vowed to purify Libya "inch by inch, house by house, room by room, alley by alley" — "*zenga zenga*" in Qaddafi's pronunciation of the Arabic word for "alley" — "person by person."

No sooner did Qaddafi's address end than the gunfire in Misurata significantly escalated. "It was like the security forces had been awaiting orders for what to do," Majdi said. "After the speech, they just opened up everywhere."

The cadets remained quarantined; they were besieged by elements outside the compound

walls whose goals they weren't allowed to know and kept within those walls by soldiers who clearly didn't trust them. As the days passed and the unseen gun battles raged, the students lounged around their barracks wondering what was to become of them. It was virtually all Majdi el-Mangoush and Jalal al-Drisi could talk about. "We would sit together for hours and go over every little detail, every clue we had picked up," Majdi said. "'What did it mean? Did it mean anything?' But sometimes it got to be too much. We had to stop. We had to talk about football or girls, anything to distract us."

Their peculiar limbo ended on the night of Feb. 25, when soldiers of the elite 32nd Brigade suddenly appeared on the base. Announcing that they had come from Tripoli to "rescue" the cadets, the commandos ordered the students to gather their things and run to a gathering point at the edge of the compound where buses were waiting.

Someone in the vaunted 32nd had made a logistical error, however. To transport the 580 cadets, just two buses had been ordered. With each vehicle filled to bursting, the excess students were crammed wherever they might fit in the brigade's jeeps and armored cars, and then the convoy trundled into the night for the long journey to Tripoli.

Beyond effecting their "rescue" from Misurata, the regime in Tripoli didn't really seem to know what to do with its young charges either. Bused to a vacant military high school compound on the southern outskirts of the city, the cadets were billeted in barrack halls and empty classrooms but barred from leaving or having any contact with their families. That edict was enforced by armed soldiers posted at the gates.

But the confines of the Tripoli high school were a good deal more porous than those of the air force academy, and from their minders the cadets gradually learned something of the conflict that had befallen their nation. Although the unrest was fomented by criminal gangs and foreign mercenaries in the hire of Libya's Western enemies, they were told, misguided segments of the population had joined in to spread it. By the beginning of March, this foreign-spawned criminality was most intense in Misurata and Benghazi, and both cities had become pitched battlegrounds.

Provided with this narrative, Majdi was not altogether surprised when, in mid-March, Western alliance warplanes began appearing over Tripoli to bomb government installations. It seemed merely to confirm that the nation was being attacked from beyond. Naturally, the situation also caused both Majdi and Jalal to worry about the fate of their hometowns and wonder which of their friends might have been seduced into joining the traitors' ranks. "That's something we talked about a lot," Majdi said. "'Oh, Khalid was always a little crazy; I bet he's gone with them.'"

The cadets seemed gradually to win the trust of the regime, enough for one large group to be transferred to a military base in mid-April to begin training on missile-guidance systems. Neither Majdi nor Jalal were selected for this mission, however, and their stay at the high school dragged on. Then one day in early May, Majdi ran into an old acquaintance at the barracks. The acquaintance, Mohammed, was now a military intelligence officer. He wanted to talk to Majdi about Misurata. The two chatted for some time, with Mohammed asking about different locations in the city and if the young cadet might know who the town's "civic leaders" were. Majdi thought nothing of the conversation, but one afternoon a few days later, he was called to headquarters.

There, an officer informed Majdi that he had been selected to join the cadets undergoing missile-guidance training; the jeep that would transport him to the base was leaving immediately. So hurried was his departure that Majdi didn't even have time to say goodbye to Jalal.

But the jeep driver didn't take him to the army base. Instead, he followed the Tripoli ring road to the coastal highway and then turned east.

By early evening, they had reached Ad Dafiniyah, the last town before Misurata and the farthest limits of government control. There, Majdi was led into a small farmhouse, where he was told someone wanted to speak to him on the phone. It was Mohammed, the military intelligence officer.

As Mohammed explained, the young air force cadet had been chosen for a "special patriotic mission": He was to slip into Misurata and find out who the rebel leaders were and where they lived. Once he had done this, he would pass the information to a liaison officer secreted within Misurata, a man named Ayoub. To make contact with Ayoub, Majdi was given a Thuraya satellite phone and a number to call.

Upon hearing all this, Majdi had two thoughts. One was about his friends at home: Ever since hearing about the scale of fighting in Misurata, he assumed that some of his friends must have joined the other side. If he carried out this mission, it might very well result in their deaths.

The other thought was of a recent conversation he had with Jalal. His friend had awoken in a despondent state of mind, explaining that he'd had a terrible dream, and it took Majdi some time to coax out the details. "I dreamt that you and I were sent to fight in Misurata," Jalal finally revealed, "and that you were killed."

But any hesitation swiftly passed. In his goldfish-bowl existence in Tripoli, Majdi had heard only what the regime wanted him to hear, and if he didn't believe all of it, he believed enough of it to want to help defeat the foreigners and their followers who were destroying Libya, even if this included people he knew. Perhaps most of all, he just wanted the limbo to end. For nearly three months, he had been cut off from both his family and the outside world, and he simply wanted something — anything — to happen. So he agreed.

Early the next morning, Majdi said goodbye to his companions at the farmhouse and headed alone into no man's land. Misurata lay some 10 miles to the east. In the right front pocket of his pants he carried his military identification card. If stopped by the rebels, this card in itself was unlikely to cause him problems; countless government soldiers had deserted, and the fact that Majdi was from Misurata would certainly lend credence to his explanation that he was trying only to go home. The satellite phone in his left pocket was a very different matter, though. With the severing of internet and cellphone reception, the Thuraya had become the standard mode of communication for regime operatives in the field, and if the rebels discovered Majdi's — sure to be found in the most cursory of searches — they would inevitably conclude that he was coming into Misurata as a spy. Under those circumstances, summary execution was probably the most merciful outcome he could hope for.

As he walked, the sound of gunfire grew in intensity, and there was the occasional rumble of distant artillery explosions. But between the light wind and the rolling-hill topography of the Misurata coastal shelf, it was quite impossible for Majdi to determine how close any of it was or even its direction. He tried to bear in mind something he picked up in basic training, that the most worrisome noise on a battlefield wasn't gunshots but rather a soft popping sound, like the snapping of fingers. This was the sound the air made as it rejoined behind a bullet, and you heard it only when a bullet passed close to your head.

Majdi's memory of that journey is vague. He doesn't remember how long it took; he estimates that he walked for about three hours, but it could have been shorter or twice as long. Only one moment sticks out in his mind. About halfway across no man's land, Majdi was suddenly filled with a sense of joy unlike anything he had ever experienced before.

"I can't really describe it," he said, "and I've never had a feeling like it since, but I was just so happy, so completely at peace with everything." He fell silent for a time, groping for an explanation. "I think it's because I was in the one place where I was out from the shadow of others. I hadn't betrayed my friends yet, I hadn't betrayed my country yet — that is what lay ahead — so as long as I stayed out there, I was free."

14.

Majd Ibrahim
Syria

LIKE MAJDI EL-MANGOUSH in Libya, Majd Ibrahim was at first merely a long-distance observer of the deepening turmoil in the region. The Syrian dictatorship made no attempt to conceal the revolts in Tunisia and Egypt from its people, and indeed spoke of them openly, with a certain smugness. "We have more difficult circumstances than most of the Arab countries," President Bashar al-Assad grandly informed The Wall Street Journal on Jan. 31, "but in spite of that, Syria is stable. Why? Because you have to be very closely linked to the beliefs of the people."

Shortly after that interview, however, Syria's state-controlled media went silent on the whole topic. Certainly there was scant mention when, in early March, demonstrators took to the streets of the southern Syrian city Dara'a to protest the arrest and reported torture of a group of high-school students for writing anti-government graffiti on walls. "I heard about what happened in Dara'a through social media," Majd said, "from Facebook and YouTube."

It was from the same venues that Majd learned of a solidarity protest, called the Day of Dignity, that was to take place in front of the Khaled bin al-Waleed Mosque in downtown Homs on March 18. Heeding the admonitions of his parents, Majd stayed well away from that rally, but he heard through friends that hundreds of demonstrators had shown up, watched over by a nearly equal number of police officers and state security personnel. It was a shocking story to the 18-year-old college student; Homs had simply never experienced anything like it.

And that demonstration was tiny in comparison with the next, held a week later. This time, the protesters numbered in the thousands. Majd, figuring there was safety in numbers amid the throngs of onlookers, managed to get close enough to hear their demands: for political reform, greater civil rights, a repeal of the state-of-emergency edict that had been in place in Syria for the previous 48 years.

On March 30, Assad delivered a speech to the Syrian Parliament, carried live by state television and radio outlets. While protests had spread to a number of Syrian cities, they were still largely peaceful, with dissenters calling for changes in the regime rather than for its overthrow. As a result — and with the assumption that the regime

had learned something from the recent collapse of the Tunisian and Egyptian governments and the widening chaos in Libya — many expected Assad to take a conciliatory approach.

That expectation was also based on Assad's personality. In the 11 years he had ruled the nation since the death of his father, the unassuming ophthalmologist had adopted many trappings of reform. With his attractive young wife, the British-born Asma, he had put a pleasing, modern face on the Syrian autocracy. Behind the charm offensive, however, little had truly changed; Syria's secret police were still everywhere, and the "deep state" — the country's permanent ruling class of bureaucrats and military figures — remained firmly in the hands of the Alawite minority. The Alawites, along with many in Syria's Christian minority, feared that any compromise with the protesters was to invite a Sunni revolution and, with it, their demise.

After offering vague palliatives about future reform, Assad instead used his parliamentary speech to accuse the troublemakers in the streets of aiding the "Israeli enemy" and to issue a stern warning. "Burying sedition is a national, moral and religious duty, and all those who can contribute to burying it and do not are part of it," he

declared. "There is no compromise or middle way in this." In keeping with a tradition begun during his father's reign, Assad's speech was repeatedly interrupted by members of Parliament leaping to their feet to shout out their undying love and gratitude to the president.

In Majd's memory, a kind of uneasy quiet fell over Homs after Assad's address. There were still scattered protests about town, watched over by phalanxes of heavily armed security forces, but it was as if no one was quite sure what to do next — each side fearful, perhaps, of leading the nation into the kind of open warfare then roiling Libya.

The interlude ended abruptly on April 17, 2011. That evening, as reported by Al Jazeera, a small group of demonstrators, maybe 40 in all, were protesting outside a mosque in Homs when several cars stopped alongside them. A number of men clambered out of the cars — presumably either local plainclothes police officers or members of the largely Alawite *shabiha* — and proceeded to shoot at least 25 protesters at point-blank range.

It was as if gasoline had been thrown on a smoldering fire. That night, tens of thousands of demonstrators gathered at Clock Tower Square downtown, and this time, the police and *shabiha* took to the roofs and upper floors of the surrounding buildings to shoot down at them. "That is when everything changed," Majd said. "Where before it was protests, from April 17 it was an uprising."

As protesters started to be killed almost every day, their funerals the next day became rallying points for more protesters to take to the streets; the evermore brutal response of the security forces at these gatherings then created a new round of *shaheeds*, or martyrs, ensuring greater crowds — and more killing — at the next funerals. By early May, the cycle of violence had escalated so swiftly that the Syrian Army came into Homs en masse, effectively shutting down the city.

"Nobody trusted the local security forces," Majd recalled, referring to the vast apparatus of *mukhabarat* and uniformed police who traditionally held sway in Syrian towns. "But everyone liked the soldiers coming in. Even I did, because we believed they had come to protect the people and stop the killing. And it worked. The army had tanks and everything, but they didn't use them, and very soon the killing ended."

After just a short time, however, the regime withdrew the bulk of its military forces from Homs in order to deploy them on "pacification" operations elsewhere — and with the army no longer able to provide order, the *mukhabarat* began distributing heavier weapons to the semiofficial *shabiha*. The city swiftly fell back into bloodletting. Around Homs, vigilante forces set up roadblocks and conducted raids into neighborhoods now controlled by the rebels. Throughout the summer the fighting continued, with different factions of pro- and anti-regime gunmen taking control of ever more sections of the city.

Then matters took an even more sinister turn. In this most religiously mixed of Syrian cities, suddenly people began turning up dead for no other discernible reason than their religious affiliation. In early November 2011, according to an unconfirmed account from Reuters, gunmen stopped a bus and murdered nine Alawite passengers. The next day, at a nearby roadblock, Syrian security forces, seemingly in retaliation, led 11 Sunni laborers off to be executed. All the while, a terror campaign of kidnappings and assassinations targeted the city's professional class, leading many of them to go into hiding or flee.

The fighting also had a surreal inconstancy. Some districts saw scorched-earth battle, even as, in others, shops stayed open and the cafes were full. Throughout, Majd Ibrahim continued his hotel-management courses at Al-Baath University. His neighborhood, Waer, remained one of the least affected by the violence, and by carefully monitoring the news for reports of specific conflagrations, he was able on most days to navigate the two-mile journey to his campus. By February 2012, however, the combat had become so indiscriminate that the university announced it was

temporarily closing. At the same time, rumors began circulating through Homs that the Syrian Army would be returning in force, this time to put down the rebellion once and for all.

"That's when my parents decided to send me to Damascus," Majd explained. "With the university closed and the fighting about to get worse, they felt there was no reason for me to stay — and it was going to become especially dangerous for young men." When Majd left for the Syrian capital in early February, he passed a seemingly endless line of army transport trucks, tanks and artillery pieces parked on the shoulder of the highway just outside Homs. The next day, the Syrian Army moved in.

15.

Majdi el-Mangoush
Libya

THE FIRST LIVING soul that Majdi el-Mangoush saw upon reaching Misurata's western outskirts was a young boy, perhaps 8 or 9, playing in the dirt. The homes all around were deserted and shell-pocked, but then he noticed a car parked in the shadow of a farmhouse wall.

"Is your father here?" Majdi asked the boy. "Will you take me to your father?"

At the farmhouse, he met the boy's father, a man in his 30s, who was both astonished and deeply suspicious of this stranger emerging from no man's land. Majdi repeated his cover story: that he had deserted from the regime and was trying to reach his family. He was helped in this subterfuge by his surname, for everyone in Misurata knew of the Mangoush clan. The man's wariness eased off, and he offered Majdi a lift into town.

As much as he'd heard about the fighting in his hometown, Majdi was unprepared for the reality. Since late February 2011, Misurata had been increasingly under siege by government forces, its residents becoming almost wholly dependent on whatever food and medical supplies could be brought in by sea. All the while, the army had rained down artillery shells, while its soldiers fought the rebels alley by alley, person by person, just as Qaddafi had promised. The siege abated somewhat with the advent of Western alliance airstrikes in late March, but the damage done to the city was staggering. Everywhere Majdi could see buildings blasted by tank shells or scorched by fire, destruction so great that in some places he couldn't even tell which street or intersection they were passing.

The man from the farmhouse dropped Majdi off at his family's home. "I just came through the front door," he recalled. "The first person I saw was my sister. And then there were my sister-in-law

and my brother's children." At the memory, Majdi blinked back tears. "It had been three months. I thought I would never see them again."

Majdi spent the rest of that day in reunion with his family. He learned that after his father became seriously ill, his parents had gone out aboard a medical evacuation ship to Tunisia. He also learned that the list of local "traitors" to the regime didn't just consist of old friends but extended to his own family; in fact, for several weeks, his oldest brother, Mohammed, had secreted a group of deserting air force helicopter pilots in his own home. Everyone, it seemed, had joined the revolution and was now committed, after all Misurata had suffered, to see it through to the finish.

At some point during this family gathering, Majdi briefly excused himself to go to his old bedroom. There, he took the Thuraya from his pocket and hid it on a shelf behind a bundle of bedding. "I didn't know what I was going to do yet," he said. "I just knew that I had to hide that phone."

Over the next week, the returned son of Misurata wandered about his ruined city, meeting up with friends and learning of those who had been wounded or killed in battle. In the process, he came to see that everything he had been told and had believed about the war was a lie. There were no criminals, there were no foreign mercenaries — at least not among the rebels. There were only people like his own family, desperate to throw off dictatorship.

But this realization placed Majdi in a very delicate spot. Ayoub, his intelligence contact, surely knew of his arrival in Misurata and was expecting him to report in. Majdi briefly entertained the idea of simply discarding the Thuraya and going on as if nothing had happened, but then he thought of the repercussions that would befall his family if the regime won out in the end. Or what if the rebels uncovered the regime's spy cell in the city and his name surfaced?

Faced with these possibilities, the air force cadet came up with a far more clever — and dangerous — plan. In mid-May, he presented himself to the local rebel military council and revealed all. As Majdi well knew, for a would-be spy to throw himself on the mercy of the enemy in wartime is never a good bet — the rebels' most expedient path would be to imprison or execute him — but against this outcome, he made a bold offer.

The next morning, Majdi finally contacted Ayoub, his regime handler, and agreed to meet two days later in a vacant apartment building downtown. At that meeting, a group of rebel commandos burst in with guns drawn and quickly wrestled both men to the ground. Majdi and Ayoub were then placed in different cars for transport to prison. By the time the rebel military council announced that it had captured "two regime spies" in Misurata, Majdi was already back at his family home.

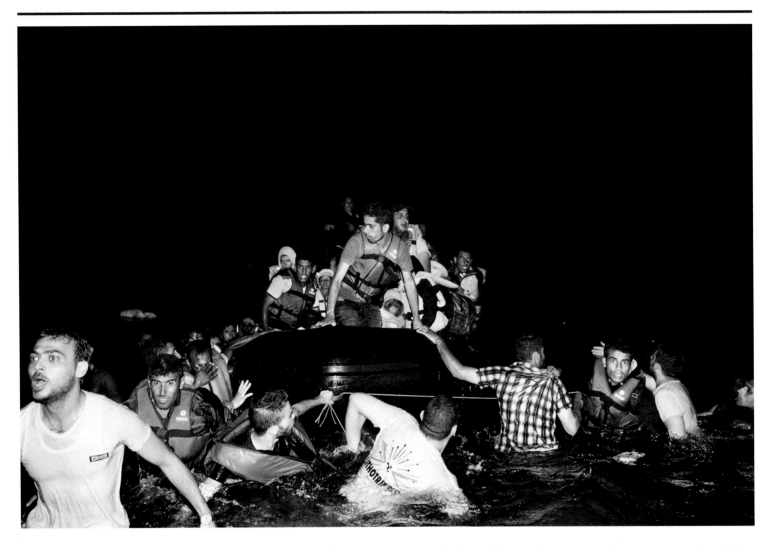

Although the sting had come off perfectly, there were apt to be other regime operatives aware of Majdi's assignment, making it risky for him to move about the city. He took advantage of the moment to slip off to Tunisia to visit his parents.

For Majdi, then 24, the contrast of Tunisia — modern, peaceful — was yet another journey into bewilderment. "It was so quiet, so relaxed," he recalled, "that it took me some time to believe it was real."

Majdi might easily have stayed on in Tunisia; it's certainly what his parents wanted. But after a few weeks, he grew restless, gnawed by a sense that his role in his country's war wasn't complete. "I think part of it was a kind of revenge. I had been with the army, but they had lied and manipulated me. And, of course, the war wasn't over yet; people were still fighting and dying. I told my parents I had no choice. I had to go home."

Back in Misurata, Majdi immediately became active with a local rebel militia, the Dhi Qar Brigade, for the march on Qaddafi's redoubt in Tripoli. Before he could be deployed there, however, the government forces in the capital collapsed, and the dictator and his remaining loyalists retreated down the coast to Surt, Qaddafi's tribal homeland district. There, surrounded and with their backs to the sea, they waged a desperate last stand. For a month, Majdi's unit held a stretch of the Surt bypass highway, shelling regime strongholds and engaging in the occasional firefight whenever the trapped soldiers tried to break out. As elsewhere in the Libyan war — as in most wars, frankly — combat in Surt was an oddly desultory affair, moments of intense action followed by long stretches of tedium, and to Majdi it seemed this rhythm might continue indefinitely.

Instead, it ended very suddenly on Oct. 20, 2011. That morning, a fierce firefight erupted in the western part of Surt, punctuated by a series of airstrikes from Western coalition warplanes; from his perch on the bypass road, Majdi saw enormous plumes of fire and dust rising up from the bombs exploding around the city. Around 2 p.m., there came another concentrated flurry of small-arms fire from the western suburbs, one that lasted about 20 minutes, before all fell quiet. Initially, Majdi and his comrades thought it meant that Qaddafi's men had surrendered, but there soon came even better news: The dictator himself had been captured and killed. "We all cheered and hugged each other," Majdi recalled, "because we knew it meant the war was over. After all that killing — and after 42 years of Qaddafi — a new day had finally come to Libya."

With the fighting at an end, Majdi returned to Misurata and transferred to a militia unit more suited to his gentle character: an ambulance crew ferrying the more severely war-wounded from Misurata's hospitals to the airport for advanced medical treatment abroad. He greatly enjoyed this work, which he felt showed tangible evidence of recovery after so much death and devastation, and it fortified his optimism about the future.

Then one December day at the Misurata airport, Majdi received a visitor. He was Sameh al-Drisi, the older brother of his friend Jalal, and he had traveled the 500 miles from Benghazi to ask a favor. The Libyan revolution had been over for two months, but the last time anyone in the Drisi family had heard from Jalal was in May. That communication was a short phone call from the Tripoli high school where the air force cadets had been sequestered, and it came just days after Majdi left for his spying mission to Misurata.

Changing course once again, Majdi set out in search of his lost friend with a tenacity that bordered on obsession. Returning to Tripoli, he spent weeks tracking down some of their former academy classmates and, from them, was able to piece together at least part of the mystery. In May 2011, Jalal had been among a group of some 50 cadets at the Tripoli high school who were assembled and told they were being sent to assist front-line troops as they advanced on the rebels in Misurata, checking for old booby-traps and guarding communication and supply lines. Instead, the cadets were used as bait there, sent out over open ground to be shot and shelled at, while the regime's more seasoned soldiers sat back to observe where the enemy fire was coming from. As one cadet after another fell on this suicide mission, Jalal and two of his comrades managed to reach an outlying farm, where they begged an old farmer to take them south, away from the battlefield; instead, the farmer betrayed the students and delivered them to internal security forces, who in turn delivered them right back to the army. After a round of beatings, the three were sent back to their suicide squad.

But that was as far as the tale went. Shortly after, Jalal's two companions had made a second escape attempt — this time successfully — but by then Jalal had been moved to a different part of the front.

This set Majdi off on a new search. He finally found another former classmate who completed the story. One day in June, a small group of the cadets — Jalal and others who had managed to survive that long — were bivouacked along a farm road on Misurata's southern outskirts when an officer drove up and called the students over for a situation report. In that same moment, a missile from an unseen Western alliance warplane or drone blew apart the officer's car, instantly killing him and most of the cadets standing nearby. When the missile struck, Jalal was sitting beneath a tree some 50 yards away, but it was there that an errant piece of shrapnel found him, tearing off the top of his head. His surviving companions buried Jalal's spilled brain beneath the tree but put his corpse in a truck with the other dead for transport to some unknown cemetery.

"Of course I was reminded of the dream he'd had," Majdi said. "Yes, we'd both gone to Misurata to fight, but it was he who died."

For most people, this might have meant an end to the search, but not Majdi. Recalling the time he had spent with Jalal's family in Benghazi, the hospitality they had shown him, he was determined to find his friend's body so that it might be returned to them. After knocking on the doors of countless functionaries in the new revolutionary government, he was finally directed to a Tripoli cemetery where the "traitors" — that is, Qaddafi regime loyalists — had been gathered up and buried.

It was a grim, trash-strewn stretch of land dotted with hundreds of graves. Majdi methodically passed down each row, but Jalal's name wasn't listed. Finally, he came to a far corner of the cemetery where he saw a grave marked "unknown." Majdi felt a burst of excitement, for it occurred to him that given Jalal's terrible head wound, identification might have been impossible — but then he noticed three more graves with the same "unknown" markers. Returning to the cemetery office, he asked for the photographs taken of the unidentified corpses before burial: The faces of all four were so horribly damaged as to be unrecognizable.

Still, Majdi was now convinced that one of the four was Jalal. He broke the news to the Drisi family and several months later flew to Benghazi to pay his respects to them in person. "It was a very emotional meeting," he said, "and I apologized to them for not being able to watch out for Jalal, but. ..." He drifted off in sadness for a moment, but then abruptly righted himself. "So that is it. Jalal is in one of those four graves, that is for sure."

16.

Majd Ibrahim
Syria

MAJD SPENT THREE months in Damascus as street battles raged throughout his hometown, and even though the atmosphere in the capital was tranquil — disconcertingly so — he was eager to get back to his family and his studies. Finally in May 2012, the situation in Homs had sufficiently calmed to allow the university to reopen.

Majd had kept in regular contact with his parents and friends during his Damascus stay, so he knew that the fighting in Homs had been centered in the Baba Amr neighborhood south of downtown. He'd been told that the damage was extensive, but he wasn't prepared for the reality. "We drove past it on the day I got back," he recalled, "and — well, it was just gone. Everything was gone. I remember thinking — trying to find something positive, you know? — Everyone should come see this. If people saw Baba Amr now, maybe it would be a lesson. They would understand how terrible war is." The naïveté of that notion soon became obvious; within weeks of Majd's return, the battle for Homs started up in earnest again. This time, the regime was targeting the insurgents in the Khalidiya neighborhood, and because the army's main artillery staging ground was next to the Waer district, it meant shells passed directly over the Ibrahims' apartment building at all hours.

"When they went overhead," Majd said, "it was like the air was sucked away. I don't know how else to describe it, but you felt it in your lungs. It was hard to breathe for maybe a half-minute afterward, like all the oxygen was gone."

The fighting in Homs raged on through the summer of 2012, with the Syrian military methodically targeting one rebel-held neighborhood after another, their ground-troop assaults backed up by tanks, artillery and helicopter gunships. Throughout, though, the middle-class neighborhood of Waer remained an oasis of comparative calm. Majd attributed it to Waer's diversity; with its mixed population of Sunnis, Alawites and Christians, none of the rebel militias could truly control the enclave — and if the militias weren't there in force, the overextended Syrian Army couldn't be bothered.

By the autumn of 2012, that began to change. On the streets of Waer, Majd noticed more and more young men toting weapons, and of those who wore insignia, by far the most common was that of the Free Syrian Army, or F.S.A. The militiamen also took notice of Majd. Of perfect combat age at 20, he found his daily ventures to the university growing ever more stressful as the gunmen demanded to know who he was allied with or taunted him for not "joining up."

In response to the growing tension in Waer, the Ibrahims began renting a "shelter home" — a safety measure that many of the city's more affluent residents were adopting. By now, so many families had fled Homs that furnished apartments sat empty throughout the city. Contacting one such family that had left for Damascus, Majd's father arranged to rent their apartment in an outlying neighborhood for use whenever trouble cropped up in Waer. At first, the Ibrahims decamped to their shelter home only occasionally, but by early 2013 their flights had increased in frequency to two or three times a week. Their greatest concern was for the safety of their eldest son at the hands of the militias.

"Most of them were just guys from the neighborhood who'd managed to get their hands on some guns," Majd explained. "I knew a lot of them — I'd grown up with them — so that was good. But more and more were coming in from the outside, and those guys were tough. A lot of them were survivors of the battles in Baba Amr and Khalidiya. They were suspicious of everyone, and you just never knew what they were going to do."

Adding another unsettling element to the mix, a lot of the fighters were on drugs, habitually popping an amphetamine called Captagon that could keep them alert for days, counteracted by an anti-anxiety drug called Zolam to bring them down.

Of all the various armed groups that had pitched up in Waer — and many were little more than neighborhood self-defense committees — the Free Syrian Army spurred a particular disdain in Majd. While many in American foreign-policy circles were professing to see secular progressives who, if supported, might lead Syria to democracy, Majd saw only a bunch of opportunists and cowards.

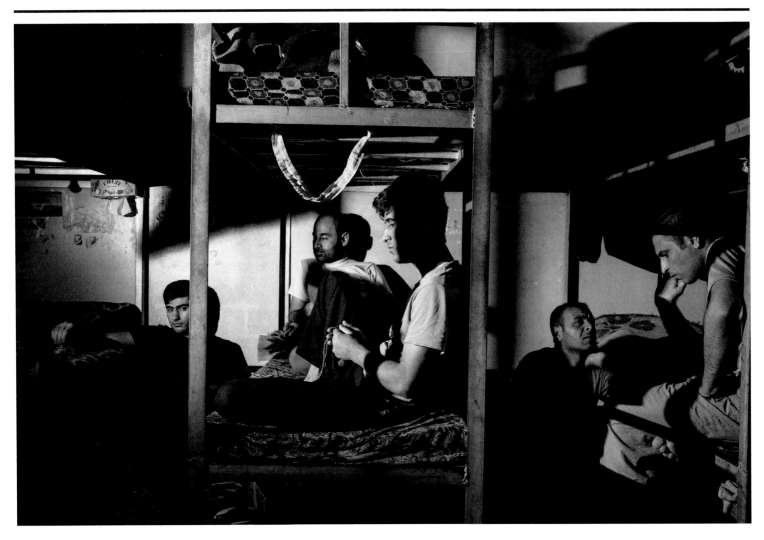

"At least the guys in the Islamist groups had some beliefs and discipline," he said, "but most of the F.S.A. in Waer were just young guys who wanted to walk around with guns and scare people. And the funny thing about that is they were the ones who scared very easily. If another group came into their area, they would just turn around and join that group."

One day, Majd came upon a young F.S.A. commander he'd come to know quite well, an incessant chain-smoker, sitting dejectedly and cigarette-less. When Majd asked why he wasn't smoking, the militiaman explained that he wasn't F.S.A. anymore. His unit had been taken over by an Islamic group that had decreed smoking was *haram*, or forbidden.

17.

Majdi el-Mangoush
Libya

IN HIS QUEST to learn the fate of his best friend, Majdi had stumbled upon a tragedy of far greater dimension. Every side in the Libyan revolution, it seemed, had taken turns killing off the air force cadets. As in Jalal's case, the Qaddafi forces had used some as bait against the rebels, but they had also executed others for simply trying to go home. In turn, the rebels, after killing many cadets on the battlefield, had executed countless more as "regime loyalists" in the flush of victory. In early 2012, scores of cadets who had survived this collective bloodletting were being held in revolutionary prisons, while many more were living in hiding. Of his approximately 580 colleagues at the Misurata air force academy, Majdi estimates that between 150 and 200 were killed during the war and its immediate aftermath.

"And we were just students," he said. "That's all we were. Both sides used us. Both sides slaughtered us."

Despite all this, Majdi was initially very optimistic about the future in post-revolutionary Libya; the country had oil, smart people and, after the 42-year reign of Col. Muammar el-Qaddafi, the will for a better life. In his view, the first great misstep was when the interim government in Tripoli, the Transitional National Council, announced that it would pay stipends to all those who had fought against the Qaddafi regime. Within weeks, the number of "revolutionaries" — approximately 20,000 by the most generous estimate — had mushroomed to some 250,000. Worse, the structure of the compensation, acquiesced to by Western governments allied with the transitional council, created an incentive for new armed groups not just to form but to remain independent of any central command, the better to demand their own share of the compensation pie. Already by the close of 2012, Libyan militias — some composed of true revolutionary veterans, others no more than tribal or criminal gangs — had begun carving the country into rival fiefs, their ability to do so bankrolled by the very central government that they were undermining. That instability was made painfully clear to the Obama administration when the American diplomatic compound in Benghazi was attacked in September 2012, leading to the deaths of Ambassador J. Christopher Stevens and three others. But for Majdi, final disillusionment took a more personal form. In the autumn of 2012, he received his "diploma" from the air force academy, announcing that he had successfully completed all the requirements for a degree in communication engineering.

"I hadn't completed anything," he said. "There

had been no classes for a year and a half, so this paper was absolutely meaningless. But this was the new Libya: Everything was just lies and corruption. And maybe I felt it more because of what I had gone through, all my friends at the academy who had been killed, but I just couldn't accept that. 'Here, take this paper. No one has to know. Call yourself an engineer.' Maybe others felt it in a different way, or they think of it more in political terms, but it was when I received my diploma that I saw the revolution had been betrayed, that Libya was a failed state."

Majdi faced a stark choice: He could use his sham diploma to land some inconsequential government job, or he could start over. The next year, he enrolled in Misurata University to study engineering. Around the time he started back at school, Majdi also became involved with an environmental group based in Tripoli called Tree Lovers. He was so inspired by its work that he helped start a Misurata branch. While both money and supplies are tight, Majdi and other volunteers have planted flowers and shrubs along many of the city's dusty median strips and sought to raise awareness about the importance of preserving the very little vegetation Libya possesses. "The desert is spreading in lots of places in Libya," he said, "and the only way to stop that is with trees."

But there may have been a more personal impulse at work on Majdi. One of the more intriguing phenomena observed among ex-soldiers most everywhere is a desire for solitude, to be out in nature, and when I visited him in Misurata, Majdi was eager to show me the forest that he and his fellow conservationists tended. On an early morning, we drove out of Misurata for the farm fields and small villages at its southern outskirts.

Majdi's "forest" proved to be little more than a few rows of scraggly pines set beside a farm road, with trash strewn about from careless picnickers, but he was very proud of it. Stepping around the garbage, he strolled among the trees and breathed in deeply of the pine scent with a satisfied smile.

18.

Laila Soueif
Egypt

FOR LAILA SOUEIF, the news of May 28, 2012, couldn't have been worse. That afternoon, Egypt's national election commission announced the names of the two men who would compete in a runoff to become the first democratically elected president in Egyptian history. There had been 13 candidates, and the only one certain to advance was Mohamed Morsi, the leader of the Muslim Brotherhood, the one party that had unified enough Islamist voters to form a meaningful

voting bloc. Against him, Laila was ready to support any of the others — save one. That was Ahmed Shafik, Hosni Mubarak's former prime minister. That afternoon, it was announced that the runoff contenders were Morsi and Shafik.

"So what to do?" Laila asked rhetorically. "Morsi was completely unacceptable, but now it was him or Shafik, so we were stuck. Well, never Shafik — that meant a return to the Mubarak era — so. …"

In just this way, Laila Soueif, the stalwart feminist and leftist, found herself backing the election of a man who advocated returning Egypt to traditional Islamic values. Many other Egyptians were aghast at the choice given to them; in the June runoff, Morsi barely squeaked in with 51.7 percent of the vote.

In his inaugural speech on June 30, Morsi promised that "in the new Egypt, the president will be an employee, a servant to the people." But a servant to the deep state may have been more accurate. Just days before the new president assumed office, the Supreme Council of the Armed Forces, or SCAF, the military junta that had ruled Egypt since Mubarak's overthrow, transferred most presidential powers to the military. That followed a decree by the Supreme Constitutional Court, a holdover from the Mubarak era, that dissolved a sitting Parliament dominated by the Muslim Brotherhood and other Islamist political parties. On the day he assumed office, then, Morsi was barely more than a figurehead, the public face to a democracy already gutted.

Morsi tried mightily to claw back the authority taken from his office. Ignoring the fiat of the Supreme Constitutional Court, he ordered the dissolved Islamist-dominated Parliament reinstated. Even more boldly, he dismissed the senior military leadership, including the powerful defense minister. In his place, Morsi promoted his own man, Abdel Fattah el-Sisi, the general who had lectured Ahmed Seif during his 2011 detention.

But then Morsi overreached — badly. In October 2012, he tried to expand the powers of the presidency by decree, a move that alarmed both the deep state and the secular opposition, already growing increasingly fearful of creeping Islamization. Morsi swiftly reeled back some of the more controversial planks in his decree, but the damage was done; in a new round of protests across Egypt, the president was denounced for trying to become a new "pharaoh" or "ayatollah."

And here was the opening the deep state seemed to have been waiting for, the chance to reopen the traditional schism that existed between its Islamist and secular opponents. For decades, the Egyptian generals had held up the Islamists — and most particularly the Muslim Brotherhood — as the greatest threat to the modern secular state and naturally positioned themselves as the guardians against them. This strategy had broken down during the heady days of revolution, with

Islamists and progressives alike turning against the generals, but Ahmed Seif had seen how easily it could be resurrected. At a meeting of human rights activists organized by Amnesty International the year before, when Egypt was still under the control of the SCAF generals, one attendee after another expressed concern about the possibility of an Islamist electoral victory. As Scott Long, an activist who was at the meeting, recalled on his personal blog, the normally soft-spoken Ahmed finally slapped his hand against the conference table. "I will not accept that the American government, or Amnesty, or anyone, will tell me that I need to tolerate a military dictatorship in order to avoid a takeover by Islamist people," he said. "I will not accept such false choices."

Now, with Morsi's overreach as president, that "false choice" was becoming increasingly stark.

"It was very clear what the state was doing," Laila said. "First, block everything that Morsi tries to do, so that nothing gets done. 'He's a failed president.' But second, feed the fears about him. That was easy to do, because the propaganda against the Muslim Brotherhood — 'They're terrorists' — went back 50 years," and the propaganda had at least some basis in reality: In the 1990s, factions of the Muslim Brotherhood had formed alliances with actual terrorists groups.

By the spring of 2013, Egypt was becoming rapidly polarized between Morsi's Muslim Brotherhood followers and nearly everyone else. Perversely, many of the same young demonstrators who took to the streets in 2011 to demand democracy were now calling for Morsi's overthrow. Even more perversely, they looked to the one state institution capable of carrying that out: the Egyptian military.

This wasn't simply a case of national amnesia. One of the more curious aspects of Egyptian society has been a longstanding reverence for its military, a tradition inculcated in Egyptian students from primary school. As a result, even during Mubarak's era, many Egyptians regarded the military as somehow apart from the venal dictatorship it upheld. Nevermind that the army was, in fact, a major beneficiary of that corrupt system — the Egyptian military owned construction companies, engineering firms, even a pasta factory — what a lot of those who took to the streets in anti-Morsi demonstrations in 2013 recalled was that the army had been instrumental in finally toppling Mubarak two years before. If the guardians of the nation had acted to overthrow one dictator, why not a second one in the making?

"You could see what was about to happen," Laila said. "Yes, Morsi was a disaster, he had to go, but to invite in the military was worse. But so many people I knew, even people who had been in Tahrir, this is what they wanted."

On June 30, 2013, the first anniversary of Morsi's inauguration, huge demonstrations took place throughout Egypt, with protesters demanding that he step down. They were met in the streets by counterdemonstrations of Morsi's Muslim Brotherhood supporters. All but invisible between these two great factions was a small group of protesters advocating a third path. It included Laila Soueif and her daughter, Mona.

"We gathered in one corner near Tahrir," Mona recalled with a rueful laugh, "and chanted, 'Not Morsi, and not the army.' People going by gave us these confused looks, like we were all crazy, and I'm sure we kind of seemed that way."

It was at this critical juncture that the defense minister, Abdel Fattah el-Sisi, until then regarded as a bland functionary, finally stepped from the shadows. On July 1, the general delivered an ultimatum to the man who had appointed him, giving Morsi 48 hours "to meet the demands of the people" or the army would step in to restore order. Pointing out that he was the elected head of state, the president defiantly dismissed the threat.

"Morsi made two great mistakes," Laila said. "First, he thought the army wouldn't move against him without the approval of the Americans. He didn't realize the generals didn't care about the Americans anymore. Second, he trusted Sisi."

True to his word, on July 3, Sisi overthrew the Egyptian government. He also annulled the Constitution, arrested Morsi and other Muslim Brotherhood leaders and shut down four television stations. Within days, he announced the formation of an interim "transitional" government, one composed of military officers and Mubarak-era apparatchiks, but all Egyptians knew that the real authority now lay with Sisi.

It was on the streets of Egypt where the face of the new regime was most nakedly revealed. In the days after Sisi took power, clashes between his supporters and those of the ousted president turned increasingly violent, with the police and the military making very clear whose side they were on. On July 8, security forces fired on Morsi loyalists gathered in central Cairo, killing at least 51. That episode set the stage for far worse. On the afternoon of Aug. 14, security forces moved in to Cairo's Rabaa Square with orders to disperse the several thousand Morsi holdout supporters who had been camped there during the previous month. By the most reliable estimates, at least 800 and perhaps more than 1,000 protesters were killed in the ensuing massacre. In an obscene parody of the 2011 revolution, hundreds took to

Cairo's streets over the following days to praise the army for its actions.

For Laila Soueif, there was to be another, far more personal indication that the new Egyptian regime was different from those that had come before.

Laila's son, Alaa, bore the dubious distinction of having been arrested by all three Egyptian governments that preceded Sisi's takeover: those of Mubarak, SCAF and Morsi. In 2006, he spent 45 days in jail for joining a demonstration calling for greater judicial independence. During the SCAF administration, he did a two-month stint in detention for "inciting violence." He fared better under Morsi, if only because the judges, Mubarak-era holdovers, detested the new president; his March 2013 charge of "inciting aggression" was summarily dismissed, while his conviction for arson resulted in a one-year suspended sentence.

Given this track record, it was probably just a matter of time before Alaa was picked up by the new Egyptian regime. That occurred on Nov. 28, 2013, when he was arrested on charges of inciting violence and, in a nice Orwellian touch, protesting an anti-protest law enacted just four days earlier. That note of black humor aside, under the rule of Sisi, matters were to play out very differently for Laila's son from the way they had in the past.

19.

Majd Ibrahim
Syria

ONE OF THE more baffling features of the Syrian civil war has been the fantastic tangle of tacit cease-fires or temporary alliances that are often forged between various militias and the regime, or even with just a local army commander. These can take any permutation imaginable — radical Islamists teaming up with an Alawite *shabiha* gang, for example — and they pose a horrifying puzzle to anyone trying to navigate the battlefield, for it means that no one is necessarily who they seem, that death can come from anywhere. But this pattern of secret deal-making also served to long inoculate the Waer district from the scorched-earth tactics the Assad regime was employing elsewhere in Homs because, at any given time, at least some of the myriad rebel militias roaming the neighborhood were apt to be in secret concord with the state.

That dynamic ended in early May 2013. In a colossal misstep, the Free Syrian Army had recently moved back into the devastated Baba Amr neighborhood, and there had been surrounded and slaughtered. Those who managed to escape the regime's cordon made for Waer and took near total control of the enclave. Sure enough, Syrian army artillery shells soon began raining down on Majd's neighborhood. While the scale of shelling was nothing like what befell Baba Amr or Khalidiya, it was enough to keep the Ibrahim family in their fourth-floor apartment, forever trying to guess where safety lay.

"You just never knew what to do," Majd explained. "Is it better here or in the shelter home? And if it's safer there, how dangerous is it to try to get there?"

As bizarre as it might seem, one reason the Ibrahims stayed on in Homs despite the ever-worsening situation was that Majd's finals were coming up at the university. Their insistence on his finishing was not some homage to the value of higher education; under Syrian law, college students were exempt from conscription, so as long as Majd stayed in school, he was safe from being drafted. Once he took his exams at the end of July, his parents decided, they would reassess the situation and decide what came next.

That gamble nearly led to disaster. On the afternoon of July 5, Majd was talking with friends on a Waer street when a white station wagon pulled up and three young F.S.A. fighters with Kalashnikovs jumped out. Grabbing Majd, they dragged him

into the car where, blindfolded, he was driven to their nearby base.

"I thought it was a joke at the beginning," Majd said. "But they knew my name, my age, what I was studying in the university. They wanted me, not anyone else."

For the next few hours, Majd's captors insisted that he admit to being a regime spy, meeting protestations of innocence with kicks and punches. Finally, he was forced to his knees, and an F.S.A. man put a large knife to his throat. Another aimed a Kalashnikov at his head.

"Well, this is the standard way they execute," Majd said softly, "so I knew this was about to happen to me. They wanted to kill me very badly."

In prelude to his execution, however, the chief interrogator thought to look through Majd's cellphone. With each phone number and photograph he flipped to, he demanded that Majd finally give up the identity of his "controller." The 20-year-old's continued professions of innocence brought more kicks, more punches. The interrogator came to the stored photograph of one young man in particular and stopped.

"Why do you have this guy's photo?" he asked.

"Because he's my best friend," Majd replied.

The F.S.A. commander slowly turned to his captive. "We will call him."

The commander left the room, and for a long time Majd remained on his knees, the knife to his throat and the gun to his head. Quite unbeknown to Majd, his best friend was also an acquaintance of the F.S.A. commander, and he came to the base to assure the militiaman that Majd Ibrahim was no regime spy. Majd learned this only when the commander returned to the interrogation room and told him he would be set free.

"So that is what saved my life," Majd said, "that photograph."

During the drive back to Waer, the F.S.A. commander started a long sales pitch on why Majd should quit the university and take up arms against the regime. Majd said he would think about it.

When he arrived at the spot where he had been picked up earlier that day, his parents and friends were waiting for him. The next morning, July 6, the Ibrahim family left for their shelter home, never to return to the Waer neighborhood where Majd had lived his entire life. It was his 21st birthday.

20.

Khulood al-Zaidi
Jordan

SINCE HER RETURN from San Francisco in 2009, Khulood had been marooned in Jordan. By 2014, she was living in a small apartment in a working-class neighborhood of eastern Amman with her

father and two sisters, Teamim and Sahar. It was a dreary place, a three-story walk-up overlooking a dusty commercial road, but it was softened by the presence of Mystery, the sisters' pet cat, and Shiny, a small box turtle they rescued from the street.

Before leaving for the United States in 2008 Khulood had briefly worked for a Japanese humanitarian organization called *Kokkyo naki Kodomotachi* (Children Without Borders), or KnK, and she rejoined the agency upon her return to Amman the following year. Her principal task was to help acclimate some of the countless thousands of Iraqi children whose families had fled to Jordan to escape the war, and so impressed were the KnK supervisors with Khulood's connection to the children that they soon hired her two sisters as well. Around the same time, Ali al-Zaidi, the retired radiologist and patriarch of the family, found work on the loading docks of a yogurt factory on the industrial outskirts of Amman. In 2014, the family was at least scraping by.

Khulood's work at KnK had undergone a shift, though. With the war in Iraq having abated, the number of Iraqi refugees in Jordan was drastically reduced from its half-million peak. They were soon replaced, however, by new refugees from the war in Syria — just a trickle at first, but by the end of 2014, their number was more than 600,000.

In certain ways, Khulood found the Syrian children quite different from their Iraqi counterparts. "The Iraqis, because they had become so tired of war, they were very peaceful and easy to work with," she said. "But the Syrian children — the boys — they have this idea, 'We have to go back to Syria to fight.' They hear this constantly from their fathers — 'You're going to be a soldier and go back to Syria' — so they're like little rebels, not little kids. It's all about home, missing home, how they need to go back and avenge what happened." By contrast, the girls had far more in common. "In both Iraq and Syria, girls are taught to keep everything inside. They aren't listened to. This makes it much harder to reach them, so their problems are deeper."

Khulood still hadn't given up on her quest to get her family out of the region. For several years, she continued to petition for the United States to reopen their case, but those efforts went nowhere. By 2014, she was holding out special hope for Britain; in Jordan, she had worked as an interpreter for a British film company, and with letters of support from her former co-workers, Khulood reasoned, the authorities there might look favorably on her. She had recently become aware of a rather diabolical Catch-22, however. Nearly the only way to win asylum in Britain — or in any other country, for that matter — was to present the petition in person. To do that, Khulood first needed to obtain a British visa, and to get that, she needed to have legal residency in Jordan. "And that's impossible," she said. "Jordan only gives residency to wealthy

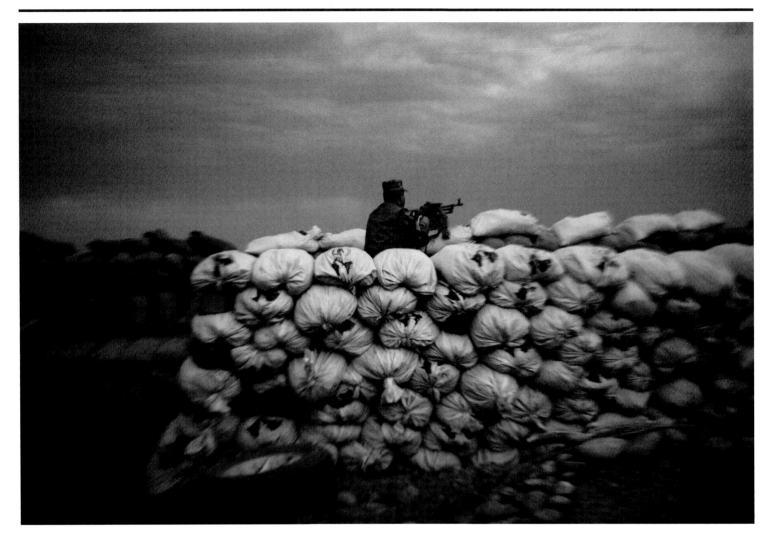

refugees who, of course, have no problem resettling in Europe anyway."

Still, in April 2014, Khulood hadn't completely given up hope. Possessed of a seemingly unconquerable will, over several days of conversation, she seemed determined to put the very best face on her situation, and she was far more interested in talking up her current plans than her past failures. Only once did this brave facade crack, and it came amid a discussion about the future she imagined for the refugee children she worked with.

"I stay with this because I want these kids to have a better life than me," she said, "but frankly, I think their lives will be wasted just like mine. I try not to think that way, but, really, let's be candid: This is their future. For me, these past nine years have been wasted. My sisters and I, we have dreams. We are educated, we want to study, to have careers. But in Jordan we cannot legally work, and we cannot leave, so we are just standing in place. That's all. Now we're becoming old, we're all in our 30s, but still we can't marry or start families, because then we will never get out of here."

Khulood sat back and let out a dispirited sigh. "I'm sorry. I try to never pity myself or to blame anyone for this situation, but I really wish the

Americans had thought more about what they were doing before they came to Iraq. That's what started all this. Without that, we would be normal."

But for Khulood and her sisters, the situation was about to grow even worse. In the autumn of 2014, Khulood said, KnK was having problems with the Jordanian government, which insisted that the organization's foreign staff members have legal work permits. While KnK said the sisters' work was exemplary, its efforts to keep them were in vain; that December, all three Zaidi sisters were dismissed from their jobs on the same day.

21.

Laila Soueif
Egypt

ON OCT. 27, 2014, Laila Soueif and her oldest daughter, Mona, climbed the short row of steps leading to the main entrance of the Egyptian Supreme Court building, then stopped and sat beside one of its stone columns. From her backpack, Laila drew out a small sign written on cardboard. It announced

she and her daughter were going to intensify the partial hunger strike they began in September to protest the injustices committed against their family. They would remain there off and on for the next 48 hours, taking no food or liquids.

"The idea wasn't to kill ourselves," Laila explained, "but to draw attention to what the Sisi regime was doing. It was the only weapon we had left." As for its efficacy, she was matter-of-fact. "A few people passing signaled that they supported us — sometimes quite a subtle signal."

Adding another layer of pain to the experience, it came at a time when Laila's family had, quite literally, disappeared before her eyes.

The first sign that the Sisi regime was to take a much dimmer view than its predecessors of dissent to its rule came with Alaa's arrest in late November 2013. Rather than being released on bail to await trial, he and his 24 co-defendants were held for the next four months. In a tactic apparently designed to break his will, Alaa's release on bail in March 2014 was followed by his rearrest three months later.

If average Egyptians were alarmed by the deepening repression in their country — less than a year after Sisi took power, there were already far more political prisoners in Egypt's jails than there had ever been under Mubarak — they gave scant evidence of it. In presidential elections that May, Sisi, now officially retired from the military, won with more than 96 percent of the vote. While this surely wasn't a wholly accurate reflection of his popularity — between those political parties that had been banned and those that boycotted the election, Sisi faced only token opposition — even an ardent opponent like Laila Soueif recognized that the former general had widespread support. She had even seen it among many of her friends and university co-workers. "They had this idea that, 'O.K., maybe he's a little rough, but he saved us from the Islamists,'" she said. "That's all they cared about, all they saw."

Up to that point, Laila's youngest daughter, Sanaa, then 20, had avoided the family tradition of run-ins with the law. On June 21, 2014, that changed. Increasingly infuriated by the treatment of her brother and Egypt's other political prisoners, Sanaa joined a human rights rally in Cairo. Within minutes, she was arrested on the same charge as her brother: violating the protest law.

Even under the tightening Sisi regime, members of the Cairene upper class like Sanaa enjoyed a degree of immunity — the main enemies of the state, after all, were the working-class followers of the Muslim Brotherhood, and they were to be ruthlessly hunted down. But when brought before a magistrate, the college student took a bold step. Despite suggestions from the judge that she stay quiet, Sanaa insisted that she had been a chief organizer of the demonstration and refused to sign her statement until this detail was included. "She wasn't going to let them do the usual thing of letting the high-profile activists go and pound on the lesser-known ones," Laila said. Sanaa, like her older brother, was held in jail pending trial.

For Ahmed Seif, Egypt's pre-eminent human rights lawyer, it had meant that his ever-expanding roster of clients now included two of his own children. At a news conference the previous January, the former political prisoner took the microphone to eloquently address his imprisoned son, Alaa. "I wanted you to inherit a democratic society that guards your rights, my son, but instead I passed on the prison cell that held me, and now holds you." By June, that haunting message applied equally to his youngest daughter.

Soon, matters took an even grimmer turn for the family of Laila Soueif. Long in frail health, Ahmed had been scheduled for open-heart surgery at the end of August; on the 16th of that month, he suddenly collapsed and then fell into a coma. Only after intense lobbying by both influential Egyptians and international human rights organizations did the Sisi regime grant Alaa and Sanaa afternoon furloughs to visit their father before he died.

"And that was the absolute worst day," Laila said, "maybe the worst day of my life. Sanaa was being held in a police station, so we had been able to see her and tell her what was going on, but Alaa had no idea. He showed up at the hospital with flowers for Ahmed, so I had to take him aside to say his father was in a coma. He said, 'So he won't even know I'm here then' and just threw the flowers out."

The day after that hospital visit, Alaa went on a hunger strike in his cell. Sanaa stopped eating also, on Aug. 28, the day of her father's funeral. A week later, Laila and Mona announced their partial hunger strike, in which they would take only anti-dehydration liquids.

In light of both Ahmed's death and the family's prominence, many observers believed that Alaa and Sanaa would be shown leniency by the courts. That belief was misplaced. On Oct. 26, 2014, Sanaa was sentenced to three years in prison for violating the protest law. The next day, Laila and Mona took to the courthouse steps for their intensified hunger strike. Laila braced herself for more bad news when Alaa went to trial the following month, by remembering something her husband had said.

"Because Ahmed had spent so much time in courtrooms and knew what certain things meant," she said, "he was always very accurate in his predictions. Before he died, when he was still representing Alaa, he told me, 'Prepare yourself, because they're going to give him five years.'"

22.

Majd Ibrahim
Syria

BY THE TIME Laila had begun her hunger strike and Khulood and her sisters were losing their jobs and Majdi el-Mangoush was back in school,

Majd Ibrahim had himself found a moment of respite — one that, although brief, had been a long time coming.

With the serial siege of Homs steadily grinding ever more of the city's neighborhoods to dust, by early 2014 even the Ibrahim family's shelter home was no longer safe. That March, the family moved once again, this time to New Akrama, a neighborhood that had been spared the worst of the violence. There, they simply waited along with everyone else for something, anything, to change.

That change finally came in May, when the last of Homs' rebels accepted a brokered ceasefire and safe passage from the city. The three-year siege of Homs was over. What had once been a thriving, cosmopolitan city was now known as Syria's Stalingrad, with vast expanses of its neighborhoods uninhabitable. It was also only then that the full horror of what some of its residents had been subjected to came to light. In the total-war environment, some residents had starved to death, while others had survived by eating leaves and weeds.

But even if a kind of peace had reached the shattered streets of Homs, the war continued elsewhere in Syria, and in a form that boded poorly for all its citizens. Majd Ibrahim heard the names of so many new militias competing with the plethora of already existing ones, it was quite impossible to keep track of them all. For sheer daring and cruelty, however, one group stood out: the Islamic State, or ISIS.

An even more radical offshoot of Al Qaeda, the newcomers attracted Islamic extremists from around the world. In Syria, the group announced its presence with a series of sudden, brutal attacks in Aleppo and the desert towns to the east, battling not just the Syrian Army but also those rival militias it deemed "apostate." What most drew the attention of Majd Ibrahim was the group's reputation for complete mercilessness, for eliminating by the most horrific means possible any who would resist its will.

Just a month after the Homs siege ended, most of the rest of the world would hear of ISIS, too, when it stormed out of the Syrian desert to utterly transform the Middle Eastern battlefield yet again.

PART IV: ISIS RISING

2014–2015

23.

Wakaz Hassan
Iraq

WAKAZ HASSAN always struggled in school. "I felt whenever I tried to study, I failed," he said. At least some of his struggles might have been a result of a hearing impairment — he speaks in a loud, slightly atonal voice, often asking others to repeat themselves. But children around Tikrit were seldom tested for such things, and he simply accepted that he would never quite catch up with his classmates. After being forced to repeat a year of school, Wakaz dropped out.

By the time he was a teenager, Wakaz had joined the legions of other unskilled young Iraqi men who scraped by with day-labor construction jobs: hauling bricks, cutting rebar, mixing cement. When no construction work was to be had, he sometimes helped out in the small candy shop that his father, a retired bank clerk, had opened in Dawr, his home village just outside Tikrit. But it was all a rather meager and dull existence.

There was one potential way out. In stark contrast to Wakaz's own middling ability to find employment, his oldest brother, Mohammed, had been hired as an intelligence officer for the local security forces, and this sinecure held out considerable promise for the entire Hassan family. Given the culture of nepotism that Saddam Hussein had fostered in Iraq, and which continued to flourish after his demise, Wakaz could reasonably hope that Mohammed might someday work his way far enough up into the municipal ranks to bring his three younger brothers, including himself, into the security forces as well. But in June 2014, a series of cataclysmic events were about to break over the Sunni heartland of Iraq, and they would radically alter the fortunes of the 19-year-old day laborer in Dawr.

At the very beginning of that year, ISIS insurgents wrested control of the crucial crossroads city of Falluja in Iraq's Anbar Province, then spread out to seize a number of nearby cities and towns. At the time, Wakaz knew very little about the group, other than that it sought to establish an Islamic caliphate in the Sunni lands of Iraq and Syria. Over subsequent months, however, Wakaz, like most other young Tikriti men, had seen the elaborate recruitment videos that ISIS produced and distributed on social media. The videos depicted warriors, or "knights," as ISIS called them, clad in smartly turned-out uniforms and black ski masks as they rode triumphantly through towns they had conquered, great black flags flapping from their new Toyota Land Cruisers. Other videos from that time showed a decidedly darker side of ISIS — executions and crucifixion displays — but Wakaz claimed never to have seen those. In any event, the budding caliphate seemed far away from the sleepy and economically moribund town of Dawr.

By that June, it was far away no more. On June 6, a band of ISIS fighters entered the western suburbs of Mosul, northern Iraq's largest city, just 140 miles up Highway 1 from Tikrit. Although it's estimated that a mere 1,500 ISIS fighters participated in the attack on Mosul — and by some accounts, the number was far lower — within a couple of days, they had put the tens of thousands of Iraqi Army and security forces in the city of two million to panicked flight. By June 9, the Highway 1 bypass road around Tikrit was the scene of a frantic stampede as thousands of Iraqi soldiers, many having already shed their uniforms, sped for the safety of Baghdad, 100 miles farther south. But ISIS wasn't done. After Mosul, they quickly advanced on Baiji, the oil-refinery town 40 miles north of Tikrit, and then on June 11 rolled into Tikrit itself.

In Tikrit, just as in Mosul and Baiji, the Iraqi Army offered virtually nothing in the way of resistance, with different units seeming only to compete on how quickly they could escape and how much of their weaponry they could leave behind for the enemy. But if the army fled the region, few of the local people did. Those remaining behind included Wakaz and his brother Mohammed.

The ISIS offensive of June 2014 marked one of the most stunning military feats in modern history: In less than one week, a lightly armed guerrilla force of, ultimately, perhaps 5,000 fighters scattered a modern and well-equipped army at least 20 times its size, capturing billions of dollars worth of advanced weaponry and military hardware, and now controlled population centers that totaled some five million people. While such a colossal collapse as that experienced by the Iraqi Army must necessarily be a result of many failures — certainly, incompetence and corruption played major roles — much of it could be attributed to recent history.

Under the eight-year rule of Prime Minister Nuri Kamal al-Maliki, Iraq's Shiite majority had come to dominate most every aspect of the national government, including its military, and to lord their newfound primacy over the Sunnis. For many residents in the Sunni heartland — and this included Baiji and Tikrit — this heavy-handed treatment spawned a deep contempt for both the central government and its army, whom they regarded as occupiers. Of course, that Shiite-dominated army was well aware of the locals' contempt and deeply distrusted them in turn, to such an extent that at the first sign of trouble — in this case, a few Sunni jihadists riding into town vowing vengeance — the soldiers, fearing a mass uprising against them, simply bolted.

This was not a completely unfounded fear, because ISIS had cleverly established sleeper cells in these cities ahead of time, both to begin attacks when the battle was joined and to recruit new members to the cause. Among those recruits was Wakaz Hassan.

According to Wakaz, he joined ISIS on June 10, 2014, just as the guerrilla group became active in the Tikrit area but a full day before its attacks there began in earnest. His chief recruiter, he claimed, was none other than his brother, the 26-year-old American-trained and Iraqi-government-employed intelligence officer Mohammed. "It wasn't for religion," Wakaz maintained, "and it wasn't as if I had any emotional connection to the group — at that point, I didn't really know what they were fighting for — but because Mohammed said we should join."

Omitted from Wakaz's account was the matter of money. By the summer of 2014, ISIS was so flush with funds from its control of the oil fields of eastern Syria that it could offer even untrained foot soldiers up to $400 a month for enlisting — vastly more than an unskilled 19-year-old like Wakaz could make from pickup construction jobs. Of course, having now also seized the Baiji oil refinery, ISIS stood to turn its financial spigot into a geyser.

As pledging members of ISIS, Mohammed and Wakaz assisted in the seizing of Tikrit on June 11. The brothers also played at least a supporting role in the most horrific atrocity to occur during ISIS' June blitzkrieg.

Just to the north of Tikrit is a large Iraqi military training base still known by its American name: Camp Speicher. Thousands of cadets were undergoing training there when ISIS closed in. As might have been predicted from the conduct of Iraqi soldiers elsewhere, the regular army units and senior military command garrisoned at Speicher simply fled the compound at word of ISIS' approach, leaving the students stranded. Wakaz said he helped round up the cadets but insists he played no role in what came next.

After separating the trainees by sect — Sunni to one side, Shiite to the other — ISIS gunmen marched hundreds of the Shiite cadets to various spots around Tikrit to be machine-gunned, the mass murders dutifully videotaped by ISIS cameramen for posting on the internet. Traditionally, armies and guerrilla groups try to deny or minimize their war crimes, but not so with ISIS; when outside observers first estimated that 800 cadets were murdered that day in Tikrit, ISIS spokesmen boasted that they had actually killed many more. (The final death toll remains unknown, but estimates now range as high as 1,700.)

After the Camp Speicher massacre, Wakaz signed up with ISIS for a one-year enlistment — for a terrorist organization, it has a surprisingly formal bureaucracy — and was ferried up Highway 1 with a large group of fellow recruits to an ISIS compound outside Mosul. There, he learned the rudimentary skills imparted to new soldiers everywhere: running obstacle courses, breaking down and firing various weapons, tactical drills on maintaining squad cohesion on the battlefield. But soon enough his training took a more brutal turn.

On a morning in late June, Wakaz was summoned from his barracks by a senior commander. Instructing the 19-year-old to follow, the commander led Wakaz to a field at the edge of the compound. After a few moments, they were joined by two other men, an ISIS fighter and a civilian who appeared to be in his 30s. The civilian was blindfolded, with his hands tied behind his back, and he was crying. The ISIS fighter roughly forced the crying man to his knees, as the commander handed Wakaz a pistol. The former day laborer from Dawr knew precisely what was expected of him.

"They showed me how to do it," Wakaz said. "You point the gun downward. Also to not shoot directly at the center of the head, but to go a little bit off to one side."

In the training-compound field, Wakaz dutifully carried out his first execution. Over the following few weeks, he was summoned to the field five more times, to murder five more blindfolded and handcuffed men. "I didn't know anything about them,"

he said, "but I would say they ranged in age from about 35 to maybe 70. After that first one, only one other was crying. With the others, I think maybe they didn't know what was about to happen."

Wakaz related all this — even physically acted out how a proper killing was done — with no visible emotion. But then, as if belatedly realizing the cold-bloodedness of his account, he gave a small shrug.

"I felt bad doing it," he said, "but I had no choice. Once we reached Mosul, there was no way to leave — and with ISIS, if you don't obey, they kill you too."

24.

Azar Mirkhan
Kurdistan

DRIVING THROUGH the desert, Azar Mirkhan told me about the death of his father, Gen. Heso Mirkhan, the pesh merga warrior who helped lead the 1974 Kurdish uprising against the Iraqi government, and who then took his family into exile in Iran. When the Iran-Iraq war began six years later, Azar said, the Khomeini regime

suddenly saw a use for the Iraqi Kurd exiles in their midst and allowed Heso to resume his pesh merga leadership role, as well as his cross-border incursions. That caught up with him in April 1983, when he was killed in an ambush in northern Iraq.

"I don't really remember him that well, because I was only 8 when he died," Azar said. "My strongest memory is that there was just a constant parade of pesh merga commanders coming to our house, conferring with my father."

For nearly 30 years, Heso's remains were lost somewhere in the mountains of Kurdistan, but a few years ago Azar and his brothers began a monthslong quest to locate them. By talking with villagers and Heso's surviving companions, they finally found his bones at the bottom of a remote ravine.

"We brought them back to our village, and he was given a hero's funeral," Azar said. "Even Barzani was there" — the K.R.G.'s president, Massoud Barzani.

The doctor's sense of personal loss was more evident when he talked of the death of his brother Ali, the second-oldest of the 14 Mirkhan siblings and the first to follow Heso into the ranks of pesh merga leadership. "When Ali was killed, it was a tragedy not just for the family, but all Kurdistan," Azar said. "He was a natural leader of men — charismatic, brilliant — and, O.K., he was my brother, but I believe we would be in a very different place now if he had stayed alive. Many, many people who knew him have said this to me."

Azar told me these stories on the drive described in the preface, perhaps in part to explain why our destination, a little village in Iraq called Gunde Siba, still haunted him. He was on an indefinite leave of absence from the hospital where he worked in Erbil, the K.R.G. capital, to devote all his energies to confronting the crisis caused by the ISIS invasion. His duties, which appeared to be largely self-determined, consisted of periodically touring the pesh merga front lines and advising its commanders. Everyone in the K.R.G., it seemed, knew the Mirkhan name, and one of its happier consequences was that its bearers could expect to be treated with immediate respect and deference.

As we spoke, it became clear that Azar's self-appointed mission went far beyond confronting the threat of ISIS. He saw in the K.R.G.'s current situation a precious and unprecedented opportunity to create a true Kurdish nation. To achieve that meant not just defeating the ISIS fanatics but ridding the land of the Kurds' historical enemies, the Arabs, once and for all. "For fourteen hundred years, they have sworn to destroy us," he said. "At what point do we take them at their word?" To Azar, that point had now been reached. In his view, which is by no means a minority one in the K.R.G., the first task at hand is to sever the remaining vestiges of the Iraqi state — it is a point of pride with Azar that he doesn't speak Arabic and has only once been to Baghdad — and then to dismantle the legacy of forced Arab-Kurd integration initiated by Saddam Hussein.

Part of the doctor's severity stems from what he regards as Kurdish complacency in the face of the dangers that lay all around, and it is further fueled by the tragedy he witnessed in Gunde Siba on Aug. 3, 2014.

For 22 years after its creation in 1992, the K.R.G. was a relative oasis of stability and peace in the region, its ties to Baghdad ever more theoretical. That exempt status was most nakedly revealed during the American intervention in Iraq, in which the K.R.G. openly sided with the invaders, providing them with back bases and airfields from which to carry out the fight; as local officials are fond of pointing out, not a single coalition soldier was killed in the K.R.G. during the Iraq war. That calm continued through the steady disintegration of Iraq after the American withdrawal, as the K.R.G. became ever more reluctant to pay even lip service to affiliation with Baghdad. To the good citizens of the K.R.G., it increasingly appeared that their mountain enclave had somehow found a way to escape the maelstroms swirling around it, that the days of warrior families like the Mirkhans might go the way of folklore. That fanciful notion ended with ISIS' lightning advance into central Iraq in June 2014.

"I've never trusted the Arabs, but as strange as it sounds, I trusted Daesh," Azar explained, using a common term for ISIS. "In the past, the Arabs always lied — 'Oh, you Kurds have nothing to fear from us' — and then they attacked us. But Daesh was absolutely clear what they were going to do. They wanted to take this part of the world back to the caliphate. They wanted to eliminate everyone who was not their kind — the Christians and the Kurds and the Shia — and they were absolutely open about it. After their June offensive, I had no doubt they were coming for us next." The doctor even pinpointed where they would strike first. "Any fool looking at a map could know. It was going to be the Yazidis. It was going to be Sinjar."

The Yazidis are a Kurdish religious minority that ISIS had long excoriated as "devil worshipers" and vowed to exterminate. Their Mount Sinjar heartland was in the far northwestern corner of Iraq and outside official K.R.G. territory, making them especially vulnerable. What's more — and this is what a glance at a map made obvious — with ISIS' capture of Mosul that June, the land link between the K.R.G. and the Yazidi Kurds in Sinjar was reduced to a single rutted farm road.

In the days and weeks after the June offensive, Azar made use of his family name to compel meetings within his circle of civilian and military comrades. At each, he warned of the coming ISIS attack. "No one took it seriously," he recalled. "They all said, 'No, their fight is with the Shia in Baghdad, why would they come here?'"

On Aug. 1, 2014, ISIS guerrillas attacked an isolated pesh merga outpost in the town of Zumar, which lay just 10 miles away from the last road into Sinjar. When still there was no sign of action by the government, in desperation Azar Mirkhan rustled up five or six of his pesh merga friends, and together they raced west.

"And this is as far as we got," Azar said. "Right here."

We were standing on the shoulder of the road in Gunde Siba, just a few miles west of the Tigris River and still some 40 miles from the town of Sinjar. "By then, it was night, and right here we started meeting the pesh merga who had fled from Sinjar and, behind them, the Yazidi refugees. It was impossible to go on because the road was just jammed, everyone trying to escape. We set up a defense post here and rallied some of the pesh merga to stay with us, but this is as far as we got." He lit a cigarette and blew smoke into the air. "We were one day too late."

In Sinjar that day — Aug. 3 — ISIS began carrying out mass executions, a slaughter that would ultimately claim the lives of at least 5,000 Yazidis. They were also rounding up thousands of girls and women to be used as sex slaves. Tens of thousands more Yazidis were frantically scaling the flanks of Mount Sinjar in a bid to escape the killers. Of all this, Azar Mirkhan had only an intimation in the terror-stricken faces and anguished accounts of those survivors streaming into Gunde Siba.

But Azar had little time to grasp, let alone address, the tragedy unfolding in Sinjar. Just two days later, ISIS began a second offensive, this one aimed directly at the K.R.G. capital city, Erbil. Turning back from Gunde Siba, the doctor raced south for the battlefield.

As it happened, Azar's older brother Araz, 44, was the deputy commander of pesh merga forces along the very section of the K.R.G. frontier, Sector 6, that bore the brunt of the new ISIS assault. Azar immediately went into battle alongside his brother — but not just Araz. Most of Azar's other brothers had long since moved abroad as part of the Kurdish diaspora and had become doctors and engineers in the United States and Europe, but befitting the Mirkhan family's warrior-caste reputation, many of them set aside their businesses and medical practices to race to the K.R.G. and take up arms. At one point in that summer, five Mirkhan brothers, along with one of Azar's nephews, were fighting shoulder to shoulder at a Sector 6 firebase.

"It was a good thing ISIS didn't drop a mortar on us right then," Azar joked. "Our mother would have been upset."

But something did happen in the battle that changed Azar. After coming within 15 miles of Erbil, the ISIS advance stalled and was then thrown back by a furious pesh merga counteroffensive. During that counterattack on Aug. 20, an ISIS sniper's bullet shattered Azar's right hand. For weeks afterward, there was concern that he might lose the hand altogether, but surgery and physical therapy helped restore some function.

"The important thing is that I can shoot a gun again now," Azar said, gently curling and uncurling his fingers. "Not as well as before, but almost."

25.

Majd Ibrahim
Syria

FOR MOST OF 2014, the Ibrahim family lived in comparative safety in their new home in central Homs. With a citywide cease-fire forged that May, most new fighting had moved to the suburbs. As improbable as it might seem, the cease-fire also led to the reopening of the Safir Hotel, where Majd's father worked; beginning that September, Majd took a job serving as the Safir's receptionist. "With the cease-fire, everything was better," Majd recalled. "I wouldn't say back to normal, because so much of the city was destroyed by then, but you could see that life was coming back."

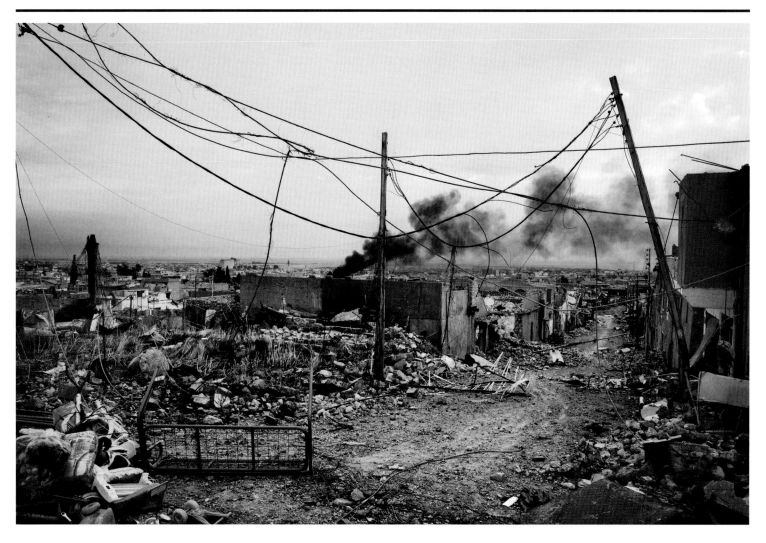

The sense of growing calm was shattered on the morning of Oct. 1, 2014. Majd was at work when he received a frantic phone call from his mother: There had just been an explosion at Akrama al-Makhzomeh, the school attended by Majd's 11-year-old younger brother, Ali, with reports of many casualties.

His mother raced to the scene, but Majd was unable to leave work for another 90 minutes. The memory of what he saw when he finally arrived at the school cast the perennially cheerful Majd into a dark corner within himself, his eyes settling into a sad, distant stare.

"Never could I have imagined something like that," he said. "It was like a nightmare, the worst nightmare. Blood everywhere, parts of children, and they're everywhere around you, and you're walking through all this — you're stepping on body parts. …" He closed his eyes briefly, struggled to control his breathing. "It's something I can just never get out of my mind."

It was only when Majd learned the details of what happened, though, that he grasped the full savagery of the attack. Just as parents and rescuers began swarming into Akrama al-Makhzomeh in response to the first blast, from a car bomb, a suicide bomber tried to enter the school's main courtyard to kill more. Shut out by an alert guard, the bomber blew himself up at the front gate. When Majd's mother reached the bomb site, she found Ali hiding with a group of terrified classmates at the back of the school.

The double bombing at Akrama al-Makhzomeh killed at least 45, including 41 schoolchildren. It was another reminder — as if the people of Homs needed one — that in the new Syria, no haven was truly safe, no place off-limits to the murderers. In its aftermath, the Ibrahim family, like almost everyone else in New Akrama, largely stayed indoors, venturing outside only when necessary.

26.

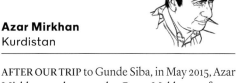

Azar Mirkhan
Kurdistan

AFTER OUR TRIP to Gunde Siba, in May 2015, Azar Mirkhan took me to the Gwer-Makhmour front, the place where he had been shot by the ISIS sniper. Venturing out to a pesh merga firebase on the forward front line, he climbed the parapet to train his binoculars on a village, perhaps 700 or 800 yards away down the hillside. All was very still there, save for two of the distinctive ISIS black-and-white flags curling in the light breeze.

A soldier called out a warning: An ISIS sniper had been spotted in the village an hour earlier, and, in his current stance, Azar made for a very easy target. The doctor gave the man an irritated look, then turned back to his binoculars.

The firebase consisted of a series of hastily constructed berms and dugouts on a ridge line about three miles from the Tigris River, with ISIS in control of the lowlands below. In the time he spent here, Azar had survived several ISIS attacks.

"First, they send in their suicide bombers in armored Humvees. If you don't destroy them as they come up the hill — and you need to make a direct hit — they blast huge holes in the walls, because these are just massive explosions. Then in the confusion of that, they send in their infantry and, behind them, the snipers. It all happens very fast: Everything quiet, and then suddenly they're everywhere. The important thing is to stay calm, to pick your targets, because if you panic, you're finished. That's the problem with the Iraqi Army; they always panic."

Panic didn't seem to figure prominently in Azar's range of emotions. "I like fighting Daesh," he said. "They're actually quite smart. It's almost a kind of game."

Perhaps not surprising in a people so implacably committed to establishing a homeland, the Kurds of the K.R.G. find it intolerable that ISIS should maintain dominion over any of their territory. Much as the United States Army will sustain more casualties in order to retrieve their battlefield dead, so the pesh merga have been willing to suffer higher losses to recover Kurdish ground more quickly.

At Black Tiger Camp, the back-base command center of Sector 6, Sirwan Barzani, the overall sector commander, could point to the enormous color-coded battlefront map on his office wall and rattle off statistics remarkable in their specificity. "When I first arrived here," he said, "Daesh was just three kilometers down the road. Now we have cleared them for 23 kilometers to the west and 34 kilometers to the south. In my sector, we have retaken 1,100 square kilometers, but we still have about 214 square kilometers to go."

By May 2015, Barzani said, nearly 120 pesh merga had died in Sector 6, where the greatest ISIS incursions had occurred. At the same time, pesh merga commanders make an interesting distinction between where they are willing to suffer losses to regain land and where they aren't. For example, the ISIS-held village that Azar studied with his binoculars was inhabited by Arabs, not Kurds.

"So even though it is on K.R.G. territory, it's not worth losing men for," he explained. "Not until we're ready to do a much bigger offensive."

But when that offensive might come was a matter tied up with international geopolitics, and with the outcome of decisions being made in Washington and Brussels and Baghdad. In light of the woeful conduct of the Iraqi Army in the past — and absent any will to place significant numbers of Western troops on the ground — many American and European politicians and foreign-policy advisers were calling for deputizing the one fighting force in the region that had proved its mettle, the pesh merga, to lead the campaign to destroy ISIS. Less clear was whether anyone had seriously discussed this idea with the Kurds.

"You know, the Americans come here, and they want to talk about retaking Mosul," Sirwan Barzani said. "Are you going to do it with American troops? No. Are you going to do it with the Iraqi Army? No, because they're useless. So let's have the Kurds do it. But what do we want with Mosul? It's not Kurdistan; it's Iraq, and why should we lose more men for the sake of Iraq?"

Animating that resistance, beyond the traditional Kurdish antipathy for the regime in Baghdad, was what the Iraqi Army collapse in 2014 brought down on the K.R.G. The Iraqis, by abandoning their American-supplied heavy weaponry and vehicles to ISIS — in most cases, they didn't even have the presence of mind to destroy it — had virtually overnight converted the guerrilla force into one of the best-equipped armies in the region, and it was the Kurds who paid the price.

By May 2015, the Americans were still trying to cobble together a workable arrangement. The response time for airstrikes against ISIS targets had greatly improved because of the recent deployment of American aerial spotter teams in the K.R.G., but much slower going was the effort to forge some kind of rapprochement between the pesh merga and the Iraqi Army. Directly beside Barzani's Black Tiger Camp in Gwer was a smaller base where Iraqi soldiers were receiving American training. "I pray for the day I don't have to see that anymore," Barzani said, pointing to the Iraqi flag flying from the adjacent base.

But Black Tiger Camp revealed something else about the K.R.G., an aspect of the society that most of its officials, whether civilian or military, try to play down or avoid speaking about altogether. For the entire time of its existence — and indeed, far predating that — the K.R.G. has been riven into two feuding camps, a schism that led to open civil war in the 1990s. On the surface, it has the trappings of a political duel between its two main parties, the Kurdistan Democratic Party (K.D.P.) and the Patriotic Union of Kurdistan (P.U.K.), but in actuality, it is a contest between two great tribal groupings, the Barzani and the Talabani. The territory's north is thoroughly dominated by the Barzanis and their tribal allies — the Mirkhans among them — virtually all of whom are K.D.P. Southern K.R.G., by contrast, is controlled by the Talabanis and their tribal allies under the P.U.K. label.

The feudalistic nature of this arrangement was on display at Black Tiger. All of the pesh merga at the camp, and along the entire 75-mile front of Sector 6, are "Barzanis," as denoted by their red-and-white tribal scarves. In the Talabani sectors of southern K.R.G., the pesh merga scarves are black and white.

Further, Sirwan Barzani is the "commander" of Sector 6 less through any military acumen on his part — before the war, he was the extremely wealthy owner of a cellphone-service provider — than through the fact that he is the nephew of the K.R.G.'s president, Massoud Barzani, who in turn is the son of the legendary Kurdish warlord Mustafa Barzani. This also explains Sirwan's impolitic frankness with a foreign journalist; as a full-fledged Barzani, he is quite beyond the reach of more temperate but lesser-named K.R.G. politicians to muzzle.

This enduring schism has had tragic consequences. In the first days of the ISIS advance into the K.R.G., the pesh merga's performance was extremely shaky, and as much as they wish to fix blame for that on the collapse of the Iraqi Army, an enormous contributing factor was that there were actually two pesh mergas, with little in the way of coordination between them. ISIS took advantage of that to nearly capture the K.R.G. capital, Erbil, and to start their extermination campaign against the Yazidis.

Time and again in the K.R.G., I detected a sense of guilt, even of shame, when conversation turned to the fate of the Yazidis. With no one, though, did I sense it more than with Azar Mirkhan. Part of that may have stemmed from his having tried to aid them at their critical hour, only to discover that the hour had come and gone. But on a philosophical level, he also felt the Kurds had betrayed their history.

"You could say that, in many ways, the Yazidis are the pure Kurds," he explained. "Their religion is what all Kurds believed at one time, not all this Shia-Sunni business. Everyone else changed, but they stayed true to the faith."

Along with his touring of the battlefronts, Azar has spent a great deal of time at the Yazidi displaced-persons camps in northern K.R.G., often working with a Kurdish-Swedish doctor named Nemam Ghafouri. These camps — some run by small independent charities, some by large international relief organizations — are home to tens of thousands of the Yazidis who outran the ISIS advance of August 2014, but when I visited in May 2015, they were being joined by a handful of others who had recently either escaped or been ransomed out from ISIS control. Despite having interviewed countless war and atrocity survivors across the world over the years, I found something uniquely horrifying about these returnees' stories. It took me some time to realize this was because of what was left unsaid, the need to puzzle out the depravity to which they were subjected.

ISIS had used rape and sexual slavery as a weapon of war to destroy the fabric of Yazidi society, and now that some of these girls and women were returning, the conservative Yazidi honor code didn't permit them to speak of what happened to them. In the company of Ghafouri, I met a 10-year-old girl whose extended family had raised $1,500 — the savings of several lifetimes — to buy her freedom the week before. She said her ISIS owners had only made her clean and wash their clothes, that they never touched her, and this was a story the family was determined to believe. I met two teenage girls who had escaped from ISIS after one month, along with a relative whom I took to be their mother — she looked perhaps 45 years old, but a very hard 45: sunken cheeks, missing teeth, graying hair — who had

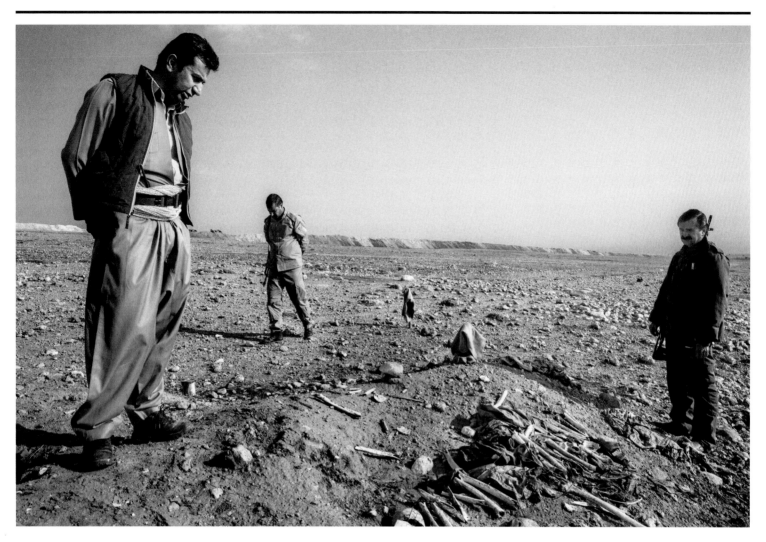

been held for eight months. Except this woman wasn't their mother; she was their older sister, and she was only 24. By her account, she had feigned deafness, which is seen by ISIS as a sign of mental illness, and in this way she, too, avoided being molested. As Ghafouri explained, her mission now was to come up with some pretext to see the 10-year-old girl and the 24-year-old woman alone. After winning their trust, she would conduct a physical examination. If they had, in fact, been raped, she would inform their families that they had some sort of infection and needed to be placed in a special hospital — no visitors — for a week.

"So then they are taken to Erbil," she explained. "They have the reconstruction — it's actually a simple operation — and they come back as virgins. Then they can be accepted back; they can marry someday. Of course it means they can never talk about what happened. They must keep it inside forever. But this is what passes for a happy ending now."

Hearing such testimonials has further hardened Azar Mirkhan's beliefs about what needs to be done if the Kurds are ever to find safety. In his view, ISIS was only the latest in a long line of implacable Arab enemies. "If this was the first time, then maybe you could say, 'Oh, it's this horrible group of terrorists.' But this has been going on for our entire history. I can promise you that when we retake Sinjar, we will go there and we will find that the Arabs stayed with ISIS," Azar said. "O.K., some are here in the camps, but many more stayed. So that is why I say our enemy is not just ISIS; it's all Arabs."

27.

Wakaz Hassan
Iraq

AT THE BEGINNING of June 2015, his one-year tour of duty with ISIS drawing to a close, Wakaz reappraised his life. Since completing his training at the ISIS compound near Mosul the previous summer, he had spent some six months back in his hometown, Dawr — his main duty there, he said, was manning an ISIS checkpoint — before being sent to fight a resurgent Iraqi Army at the oil-refinery complex in Baiji. With that battle still raging, Wakaz certainly had the option of reupping with ISIS, but he decided instead to return to the civilian world.

Part of his reason may have involved economics; with ISIS' salad days clearly over, Wakaz's pay packet often arrived late. But it most likely was rooted even more in self-preservation. Because, slowly but surely, the tide appeared to be turning against ISIS.

This was made evident to Wakaz as he contemplated just where he might go to start over. In April, the Iraqi Army, supported by American airstrikes, had recaptured Tikrit, and by that June they were closing ever tighter around Baiji. That still left Mosul and the ISIS-controlled towns in Anbar Province, but life in any of those places for an ex-ISIS fighter was sure to be grim: He would be resented by his former comrades, and a dead man should the Iraqi Army take control.

Wakaz finally settled on a very different destination: the Kurdish-controlled Iraqi city of Kirkuk.

Just as in Mosul and Baiji and Tikrit, the Iraqi Army garrisoned in Kirkuk broke and fled before the ISIS offensive a year earlier. But there the similarities ended. Racing to fill the void left by the Iraqis, thousands of pesh merga soldiers had poured into Kirkuk just ahead of ISIS and managed to throw back their advance. Ever since, Kirkuk has effectively been under Kurdish control, but the melting-pot city was also teeming with both Sunni and Shiite refugees, making it a natural hide-out for both active and former Islamist fighters. Although Kirkuk was a mere 60 miles from Baiji, the two cities were now separated by the heavily fortified line of the pesh merga army. It meant that, to reach his sanctuary city, Wakaz would have to travel the ISIS "ratline."

28.

Majd Ibrahim
Syria • Greece

IN THE SAME month that Wakaz decided to leave ISIS, Majd finally obtained his bachelor's degree in hotel management from Al-Baath University. The achievement was a mixed blessing: Now he was eligible for conscription. Before the war, a male student normally received his call-up letter four or five months after graduation, but by 2015 the Syrian Army was so depleted from defections and battlefield casualties that the call-up time had shortened to a month or two, or even just a few weeks, and there was no longer any gaming the system. When the call-up notice went out, the army might simply come to your house and haul you away. "So that was it," Majd said. "I knew that in a very short time, the army would come for me."

Just days after his graduation, Majd's parents handed their son $3,000 — all the savings they had left — and told him to leave the country.

"To them it was no longer about patriotism or defending the country," he said, "but about my staying alive." He gave a faint smile. "Plus, I would have made a terrible soldier."

On June 21, Majd's father escorted him to Damascus, where two days later he caught a flight for Turkey. Besides the $3,000, all Majd carried was whatever could fit into his small knapsack.

Hoping to stay at least somewhat near home, Majd began looking for work in Turkey. When that proved futile, he saw no choice but to join the migrant trail being negotiated by hundreds of thousands of his countrymen that summer, and so he headed west for Turkey's Aegean coast, where he might seek passage to Europe. Along the way, he serendipitously met up with an old friend from Homs whom he hadn't seen in years, Amjad, who was traveling with Ammar, another refugee from Homs. The three became a traveling team. Consequently, they shared the same overcrowded inflatable raft that, on the night of July 27, made the passage from a smuggler's beach near Bodrum, a Turkish resort town, to Kos, a Greek island several miles away.

There, Majd and his two friends endured an agonizing wait. With Kos overwhelmed by tens of thousands of would-be migrants, Greek authorities were taking up to 10 days simply to issue the registry papers that would allow their onward travel. That summer, the migrant route through Eastern Europe was becoming increasingly inhospitable, with several governments threatening to shut it down completely. Finally, Majd and his friends received their papers late on the afternoon of Aug. 4. That left them just enough time to catch the nightly ferry for the Greek mainland, the beginning of their search for refuge somewhere in Europe.

PART V: EXODUS

2015–2016

29.

Wakaz Hassan
Iraq • Syria • Turkey

ON JUNE 18, 2015, the first day of Ramadan, Wakaz bid farewell to his ISIS comrades and set off on the ISIS ratline for his return to civilian life. To reach Kirkuk, just 60 miles northeast of Baiji, Wakaz first had to travel west across ISIS-controlled Iraq and Syria, then north into Turkey, before slipping back across into Kurdish-controlled territory in Iraq — an almost complete circle of more than 500 miles. The biggest potential obstacle on this well-known route was the heavily militarized Turkish frontier.

Ever since ISIS gained strength in eastern Syria in early 2014, there have been accusations that their success relied on Turkey's keeping its border deliberately porous so that Islamist fighters from around the world might pass back and forth. That charge was made most explicitly by the Russian government in late 2015. While the Turkish administration of President Recep Tayyip Erdogan vehemently denied the charge, evidence supports the Russian account. Eleven of nearly two dozen captured ISIS fighters that I interviewed for this report claimed to have transited through Turkey at some point during their ISIS service. Nearly all of those 11 told me they encountered Turkish soldiers or police while crossing the Turkish-Syrian frontier and were simply waved through. That was certainly the experience of Wakaz.

"The man who was leading us, he went up to the Turkish checkpoint and talked to the guards for a few minutes," Wakaz said. "Maybe he gave them some money, I don't know, but then we just passed on."

As to whether there was any chance the Turkish border guards didn't grasp the affiliation of those they were letting through, Wakaz briskly shook his head. "Of course they knew. We were all young guys, and the man taking us across was Daesh. He went across there all the time. They knew."

From Turkey, Wakaz made another clandestine crossing into K.R.G. territory, and by the beginning of July 2015, two weeks after he left ISIS, he was in Kirkuk and ready for a fresh start. He was soon joined there by another ISIS retiree, his brother Mohammed.

At least initially, it seemed the Hassan brothers had chosen well. In Kirkuk, they moved into a small apartment in a neighborhood favored by other ex-ISIS fighters trying to escape notice, and within a week, both brothers found work on a nearby construction site. At that point, if Wakaz had a dream for the future, it was simply to lie low in Kirkuk, save as much money as possible, return home when the situation permitted and open his own small shop.

As modest and heavily conditional as that dream was, it ended on the afternoon of Sept. 7, 2015, when a black car pulled alongside Wakaz on a Kirkuk street. Rolling down his window, the man in the front passenger seat, an undercover policeman, asked the young man with the piercing eyes for his identification card.

30.

Majd Ibrahim
Germany

ON THE AFTERNOON of Nov. 23, 2015, I visited Majd Ibrahim at his attic apartment on the outskirts of Dresden. Provided by the local social-welfare agency, the apartment was shared by Majd and his friend from Homs, Amjad, along with six other asylum seekers, as they waited for their petitions for resident status to wend their way through the German legal system. Meals had become a new preoccupation, and two of the roommates, from India, had installed themselves as lords of the kitchen. "Their food is much better than ours," Majd explained. "They give us a list of what to buy, and we go to the market for them, but they do almost all of the cooking."

From Greece, the Syrian friends had traveled the migrant trail through Eastern Europe and reached southern Germany by mid-August. Majd had intended to continue on alone to Sweden, where he'd heard winning asylum was easiest, but those plans were dashed when the friends were pulled off a northbound train by the police. After being shunted between migrant holding facilities, they were taken to Dresden in mid-September.

For refugees from Homs to find themselves in Dresden held a certain paradox. The city, known for having been largely destroyed by Allied bombing in World War II, was also the center of the growing anti-immigration movement that had spread across Germany over the previous year. Right-wing nationalists were staging mass demonstrations in the city every Monday night. When I visited Majd, it had been just a week since terrorist attacks in Paris killed 130, and anger against migrants — and especially any from Muslim countries — was reaching a fever pitch.

"There have been quite a few incidents here just this past week," Majd told me. "A lot of the guys won't go to the city center at all right now."

Certainly they wouldn't be heading downtown that evening, a Monday, when the anti-immigrant speeches in Dresden's Theater-platz would kick off promptly at 7.

Majd spoke frequently of his intention to return to Syria; an intention that partly explained why he asked for his face not to be shown in his portrait. That afternoon I asked if he could foresee a time when such a return would be possible. He thought for a long time. "Minimum, 10 years from now," he said. "We have a saying in Syria: 'Blood brings blood.' Now everyone will want to take revenge for what has been done to them these past years, so it will just go on and on. Blood brings blood. I don't think it will end until everyone who has taken up a gun in this war is dead. Even if the killing speeds up, that will still take at least 10 years."

By coincidence, I was with Majd the following day, when, returning to his communal apartment, he found a letter awaiting him. It was from the Federal Office for Migration and Refugees, and it informed Majd that a background check had been completed and that no problems were found; it was the last major hurdle in his petition for residency, making it all but certain that he would now be allowed to stay in Germany for the next three years. Setting the letter aside, Majd crossed to one of the attic's dormer windows and sat, staring out at the street, for a long time.

31.

Khulood al-Zaidi
Jordan • Greece • Germany

BY THE END of 2015, Khulood had come up with a desperate plan. Her years of petitioning for resettlement having gone nowhere, she now saw absolutely no future for her family in Jordan. All that summer and autumn, she followed the story of the hundreds of thousands of prospective migrants making for Europe from Turkey — and, far more perilously, from Libya — aboard flimsy inflatable rafts. By December, however, it was a rapidly changing story; more and more restrictions were being placed on the migrants by European governments and, with winter coming on, the sea passage was becoming increasingly risky. As Khulood explained to her father and sisters, if ever they were to change their situation, they had to act immediately.

With Ali al-Zaidi's health too precarious to withstand the rigors of a hard journey, it was decided that Sahar would remain with him in Amman while Khulood and Teamim made for Europe. On Dec. 4, they took a flight to Istanbul and from there followed the by-now well-worn migrant trail down the Turkish coast to Izmir. After arranging to pay a smuggler 2,000 euros for spots aboard a boat, the sisters waited. The summons finally came on the night of Dec. 11.

They were driven an hour and a half down the coast. Slipping to the shoreline in the darkness, Khulood and Teamim clambered aboard a severely overloaded rubber raft — Khulood counted at least 30 other passengers, rather than the eight or 10 it was designed to hold — which then pushed off for the Greek island of Samos, a three-hour journey.

The overburdened raft lay so low in the water that twice the outboard motor died when waves broke over it. But the greatest danger came when they nearly reached safety. On the murky sliver-moon night, the pilot misgauged his approach to the Samos beach and smashed the raft against a rock outcropping; instantly, one of the air-filled pontoons began to collapse. Ready to join the other passengers tumbling into the water from the sinking boat — fortunately, all wore life preservers — Khulood thought to glance over at Teamim. Her oldest sister sat stock-still, too paralyzed with fear to react.

"I yelled at her to jump," Khulood recalled, "because the waves were very high and they were going to smash us against the rocks, but she just couldn't move. I saw that she was going

to die, but I thought, We've come too far together, we must now share our fate."

Clambering over to her sister, Khulood grabbed Teamim and somehow managed to get them both clear of the sinking vessel and onto the rocks. There they were promptly knocked down by another wave, with Teamim badly hurting her leg in the fall, but at least they were now on land. In the dark, Khulood helped her limping sister up the hillside to join the rest of the migrants as they set out in search of shelter.

The following two weeks became a blur of travel and waiting and tension for the two sisters from Iraq, an object lesson in both the callous indifference of officialdom and in the life-altering kindness of strangers. After registering with Greek authorities in Samos, the sisters were allowed to board a ferryboat for the Greek mainland and Athens, where they were sheltered by a friend of a friend. With the situation at the Eastern European frontiers changing constantly — and not in any way that augured well for the thousands of migrants still streaming north — the sisters quickly moved on. By Dec. 22, through a combination of bus, train and foot travel, Khulood and Teamim had crossed five European

borders to finally reach southern Germany.

There, their luck appeared to run out. Arrested shortly after crossing the German frontier, the sisters were held in jail until dark, then sent back into Austria and instructed to make for a refugee holding center in Klagenfurt. That camp was overflowing, however, and they were denied entry. With nowhere else to go, Khulood and Teamim simply huddled together outside the camp's gates — and then it began to snow.

Their salvation was arranged through social media. After Khulood posted notice of her situation on Facebook, a small international band of activists mobilized in search of someone in the Klagenfurt area who might help the sisters. That aid soon arrived in the form of a local Green member of Parliament, who took Khulood and Teamim to a cafe to eat and warm up. At the cafe, the politician also sent out an urgent message seeking a local family who might temporarily take in the sisters; within an hour, he had received eight offers. From the cafe, the Zaidi sisters were taken to the home of Elisabeth and Erich Edelsbrunner.

"Today is the first day we feel comfortable and relaxed," Khulood emailed a friend in England the following day, Christmas Eve. "The family is very nice. They have given us our own room. They have a very lovely dog. I love him."

32.

Wakaz Hassan
Iraq

IN DECEMBER 2015, Wakaz Hassan was being held on suspicion of terrorism in a small former police station at the edge of a village about 10 miles from Kirkuk. Along with approximately 40 other suspected terrorists, Wakaz, now 21, spent almost all his waking hours kneeling in a small and fetid room of the secret prison run by the K.R.G.'s security service, Asayish. On those rare occasions when he was taken from the communal room, he was handcuffed and blindfolded. Three months after being picked up on the streets of Kirkuk, he still had no idea where he was.

After his arrest, Wakaz quickly confessed to having been an ISIS fighter. He provided details of his service, including the six executions he carried out in Mosul. Whether this confession was coerced through torture was impossible to know — in conversation with me in the prison, Wakaz insisted that the Asayish interrogators hadn't mistreated him in any way, but even tortured prisoners tend to say that when their captors are standing over them. Over the course of our two long interviews, the young man sometimes contradicted himself, perhaps a result of trying to gauge what his questioner and captors might want to hear. That said, there seemed a core candor to his words that perhaps was at least partly because of a stricken conscience.

"I did bad things," he told me, "and I need to confess to them before God."

Shortly after his arrest, Wakaz also informed on his brother Mohammed. It took Asayish a month to track down the older Hassan sibling, and he was being held in a different prison near Kirkuk. There had been no contact between the brothers since their arrests, but Wakaz hoped Mohammed was also making a clean slate of things. His main goal now, he said, was to atone for his crimes by helping the authorities identify whichever of his former ISIS colleagues were still alive. "If I had a chance to do it over again," he said, "I never would have joined Daesh. I saw the evil things they did, and I know now that they aren't true Muslims."

Despite this professed change of heart, the 21-year-old is cleareyed about his future. "I have no illusions, and I have no hope," he told me. "I believe I will spend the rest of my life in prison."

But Wakaz was basing that belief on the fact that he had been captured by K.R.G. investigators and remained in Kurdish custody. In reality, a grimmer future was being planned for Wakaz, one plainly laid out to me by a senior Asayish officer at the secret prison.

Since the events of June 2014 — when the Iraqi Army in Kirkuk melted away before the ISIS assault, and the Kurds rushed unto the breach — the city has technically been under the joint control of the Iraqis and the Kurds. But this collaboration exists largely on paper. In practice, the Kurdish authorities have little faith in their Iraqi counterparts and see even less reason to cooperate with them on security matters. Nowhere is this separation more evident than on issues relating to ISIS.

"That's why we haven't told the Iraqis about the guys in here," explained the Asayish official. "If we did, they would demand we hand them over, since most of their crimes were committed on Iraqi territory. Then they would either kill these guys outright or, if some of them are high enough up in the Daesh leadership to arrange a bribe, let them go. We just can't trust the Iraqis at all." In light of that, the Asayish plan is to keep Wakaz under wraps and to use him to identify other ISIS fighters they capture and with whom he might have served in the field. Once his usefulness to Asayish comes to an end — and that may not be until after the retaking of Mosul and the trove of ISIS fighters expected to surrender there — Wakaz will be handed over to the Iraqi authorities. At that point, his future will be short and preordained.

"He thinks his life will be saved because we have him, and he knows we don't execute," the Asayish officer said. "But Iraq does. The Iraqis will try him in their courts, and they will give him a death sentence. Then they will transfer him to a prison in Iraq to be hanged."

When I asked if there was any chance that, because of Wakaz's assistance in unmasking other ISIS fighters, a judge might show leniency in his case, the Asayish officer quickly shook his head. Or that he could somehow cut a deal to spare his life? The officer pondered briefly, then shook his head even more forcefully.

"If he was senior Daesh, maybe," he said. "But he is a nobody and poor. So no. No chance."

33.

Laila Soueif
Egypt

IN JANUARY 2016, Laila's son, Alaa, managed to smuggle an open letter to The Guardian from his Egyptian prison cell. "It has been months since I wrote a letter and more than a year since I've written an article. I have nothing to say: no hopes, no dreams, no fears, no warnings, no insights; nothing, absolutely nothing," he wrote. "I try to remember what it was like when tomorrow seemed so full of possibility and my words seemed to have the power to influence (if only slightly) what that tomorrow would look like. I can't really remember that."

By then, Alaa was approaching the one-year mark of a five-year prison sentence, just as his father, now deceased, had predicted. It was a high price for speaking out, and one of the awful paradoxes Alaa faced — along with thousands of other political prisoners in Egypt today — was that the old way of appealing to Cairo on human rights issues no longer worked. In the Mubarak era, if enough pressure was brought to bear by the American government and Western activist groups, an Egyptian political prisoner was likely to be quietly released. If General Sisi took away any lesson from Mubarak's downfall, though, it was to never be viewed as the West's lap dog. Western pressure applied today has little effect and might even be counterproductive.

"But of course, you also can't stay quiet about it," Laila said, "because this is exactly what they want. You have to keep trying, even if it seems futile."

The obduracy of the Sisi regime on human rights has undoubtedly been compounded by a new economic reality. Today, the annual American subsidy to Egypt is less than $1.3 billion, down from more than $2 billion in Mubarak's heyday. At the same time, Saudi Arabia and other gulf states have subsidized the Egyptian government with an estimated $30 billion since Sisi took power, and given the Saudis' own record on such matters, they seem unlikely to pester their client state over issues like political prisoners or freedom of expression. The simple fact is that the West in general, and the United States in particular, now has less influence over the Egyptian state than at any time since the early 1970s.

Laila derives some perverse hope from the recent economic deterioration of Egypt, a decline so rapid and deep that it might, she believes, finally erode all remaining confidence in the present regime. "Sisi still has pools of support," she said, "but it's getting smaller all the time. The situation is really unsustainable now." But in March 2016, there were scant signs in Cairo or elsewhere in Egypt that any serious dissident movement was in the offing. "No, it won't happen today, and it won't be like Tahrir," Laila said. "I give it 18 months. In 18 months, either there will be a kind of palace coup — the generals put Sisi to one side and bring in someone more moderate — or we will come to a new wave of widespread protest. If that happens, it won't be like 2011. This time, it will be far more violent."

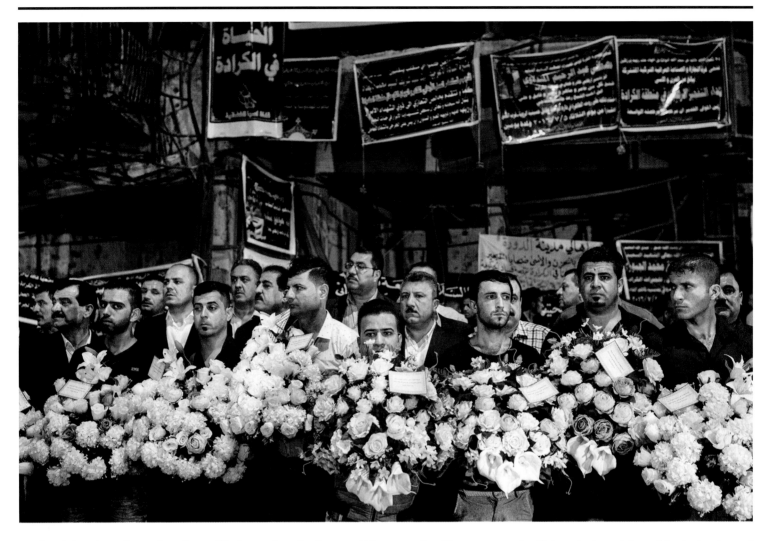

The Sisi regime shows few signs of being worried. A second case against Alaa, for criticizing the justice system on his Facebook page, is currently in court. He faces the possibility of another sentence of six months to three years. Even if prosecutors drop that case, Laila will be 64 when her son is released.

34.

Azar Mirkhan
Kurdistan

AT THE SIGHT of the Arab village on the road just ahead, Azar Mirkhan brought the car to a quick stop and swore under his breath in Kurdish. It was a poor and tattered place: off to the left, a compact cluster of earthen homes and walls and, to the right, four or five farmhouses climbing the hillside. It was the latter grouping that drew the doctor's attention.

"They're on the high ground? How was that allowed?" Azar stared darkly at the farmhouses for a moment, seething at the Arab encroachment,

then slowly turned his gaze to the village center. No residents were visible, but here and there old cars were parked in the shadow of walls.

"You see? Until two weeks ago, Daesh controlled this village, and the people living here had no problem with them, they stayed throughout. We lost four pesh merga here." Azar turned to me with his lopsided, grim smile. "You know what I would do? I would go to an Arab and ask to borrow his bulldozer. Then I'd bring in an Israeli adviser — they're very good at this sort of thing — and in two or three days, I would erase this place."

Azar has a flair for the outrageous statement, and I sometimes found it hard to know how serious he really was in such moments. But on that morning, I suspected he was quite sincere. It was Nov. 27, 2015, six months after my first visit with Azar, and we were on a back road to Sinjar, the Yazidi town that ISIS had so thoroughly savaged in the summer of 2014. In the intervening months, Azar had occasionally driven out to the pesh merga front-line trench above Sinjar to try his hand at shooting ISIS fighters — occupying an opposing trench just 40 yards away — but the pesh merga, with the help of massive American airstrikes, had recently recaptured the town

itself. Azar had participated in the battle, and this return trip put him in a dark mood.

His ill temper only deepened when we reached Sinjar. Much of the town, home to perhaps 100,000 before the war, had been reduced to rubble. While still checking for booby-traps, the pesh merga had cleared a narrow path through the ruins, and here and there lay the putrefying remains of a few ISIS fighters. So great was the damage to Sinjar that it was initially difficult to differentiate between what had been destroyed by the marauding ISIS warriors during their occupation and what had been leveled in the battle two weeks earlier, but a pattern emerged. In the small traffic circle at the center of town, ISIS had destroyed the minaret that stood there for more than 800 years. They also razed every Yazidi temple in Sinjar, along with its one Christian church. The hospital in the center of town still stood, but only because ISIS converted it into a sniper's nest and barracks, knowing that American warplanes wouldn't bomb it. Even so, they had taken the time to destroy all the medical equipment, even stomping on thermometers and glass ampuls.

It was in Sinjar's residential neighborhoods,

however, that ISIS's policy of ethnic cleansing took on an Old Testament air. On street after street, some houses remained perfectly intact, alongside others reduced to piles of broken masonry and twisted rebar. What most of the surviving houses had in common were spray-painted messages on their exterior walls, each something to the effect of "An Arab family lives here." Azar insisted that these were written not by the ISIS invaders but by the families themselves.

"This was their message to Daesh," he said. "'Spare us, we are with you, we aren't Kurds.' And just like in that village, the Arabs stayed here throughout."

Those Arab residents were now gone, having fled when American airstrikes signaled the coming battle. On several of the residential streets, some of the few Yazidis who had returned were picking their way through the Arab homes, loading looted bedding and furniture into pickup trucks.

"And why not?" Azar said. "They have lost everything."

It all became far more visceral and ghastly when two pesh merga fighters led us to a barren field a short distance out of town, near the new front lines. At the far end of the field, pesh merga engineers were cutting a tank trench — ISIS remained just a few miles to the south — but farther up, three irregular mounds flanked a seasonal water runoff. From these mounds protruded the telltale evidence of a killing field: human bones and skulls, dirt-encrusted shoes, loops of tied cloth that had been blindfolds. In the rains over the previous 15 months, some of the remains of the mass graves had leached out, so that the dry streambed was littered with women's clothes, more shoes, teeth. None of the graves had been excavated yet — the authorities were waiting for a criminal forensics team — but by best estimates, this had been the execution ground for about 300 Yazidis, most of them women too elderly to be of sex-slave interest to ISIS or children too young to be put to any use.

For a half-hour, Azar walked among the graves in silence, but I noticed he was becoming increasingly agitated and then that he was crying. I drew alongside to ask if he was O.K., if he wanted to leave. He abruptly wheeled to point a finger at the steeply rising flank of Mount Sinjar, maybe four miles to the north.

"The pesh merga were right up there," the doctor said, his voice ragged with rage. "Daesh brought them out here to kill so that we could watch. They thought about it. They did it deliberately, to humiliate us."

Returning to the center of Sinjar, Azar strode briskly into the town hall, one of the few downtown structures still habitable, and motioned for a senior official to follow him out to the terrace. For the next hour, the two men huddled in deep conversation, waving away any pesh merga underlings who thought to approach. Afterward, Azar apologized to me for having taken so long.

"I told him that he needed to destroy all the Arab homes here," he recounted, "but he was hesitant. He thinks it's better to give them to the Yazidis who return, but I said, 'No; eventually some of those Arabs will come back with their titles and deeds and try to reclaim the houses, so better to just destroy them, leave nothing for them to come back to and start over again.' He understands that now."

When I asked if he thought the official would actually follow through with the plan, Azar nodded. "He promised me. I made him promise."

That afternoon, we climbed the hairpin road that led out of town and up Mount Sinjar, the same path that tens of thousands of terrorized Yazidis had taken in their panicked flight of August 2014. All along the shoulders of the road were clumps of the clothes, faded and torn, that they cast aside as they ran.

"There used to be a lot more," Azar muttered as he looked at the detritus. "It used to be everywhere."

Cresting the mountain, we entered a broad valley plateau that extended for the next 25 miles. Scattered over the land were the tent encampments of thousands of Yazidi families that still had no homes to return to. The historic heart of Yazidi society wasn't the lowlands these people had so recently fled, but rather the very mountain on which they were now camped, and on the hillsides all around their tent cities were the remnants of their ancestral villages, old abandoned crop terraces and crumbling earthen homes. Some of these settlements had been inhabited for nearly a thousand years, but in the 1970s Saddam Hussein sent his soldiers in to destroy them as part of his anti-Kurd campaign. The mountain Yazidis had then been herded down to the lowlands where they could be more easily watched — and, of course, more easily slaughtered when ISIS rolled in four decades later.

Until a short time ago, Azar might have been derided as a xenophobe, even a fascist, for his radical separatist views. In seeing the results of ISIS's barbarism, however, and in contemplating the hatreds that have been unleashed across the Middle East in the past few years, some observers have begun to believe that his hard way of thinking might offer the best — or, more accurately, only — path out of the morass. The despair over how impossible it seems to reassemble the shattered nations of the region has caused an ever-increasing number of diplomats and generals and statesmen to consider just the sort of ethnic and sectarian separation that Azar advocates, albeit in less brutal form.

Coincidentally, the model they most often look to for how it can be done right is the Kurdistan Regional Government.

For 25 years, the K.R.G. has existed as a stable quasidemocracy, part of Iraq in name only. Perhaps the answer is to replicate that model for the rest of Iraq, to create a trifurcated nation rather than the currently bifurcated one. Give the Sunnis their own "Sunni Regional Government," with all the accouterments the Kurds already enjoy: a head of state, internal borders, an autonomous military and civil government. Iraq could still exist on paper and a mechanism could be instituted to ensure that oil revenue is equitably divided between the three — and if it works in Iraq, perhaps this is a future solution for a Balkanized Libya or a disintegrated Syria.

Even proponents acknowledge that such separations would not be easy. What to do with the thoroughly "mixed" populations of cities like Baghdad or Aleppo? In Iraq, many tribes are divided into Shia and Sunni subgroups, and in Libya by geographic dispersions going back centuries. Do these people choose to go with tribe or sect or homeland? In fact, parallels in history suggest that such a course would be both wrenching and murderous — witness the postwar "de-Germanization" policy in Eastern Europe and the 1947 partition of the Indian subcontinent — but despite the misery and potential body count entailed in getting there, maybe this is the last, best option available to prevent the failed states of the Middle East from devolving into even more brutal slaughter.

The problem, though, is that once such subdividing begins, it's hard to see where it would end. Just beneath the ethnic and religious divisions that the Iraq invasion and the Arab Spring tore open are those of tribe and clan and subclan — and in this respect, the Kurdistan Regional Government appears not so much a model but a warning.

Because of its two feuding tribes, the K.R.G. — a statelet the size of West Virginia — now has essentially two of everything: two leaders, two governments, two armies. For the moment this schism has been masked by the threat from ISIS and the desire to present a unified front to the outside world. But it remains an undercurrent to everything. It also goes a long way toward explaining the sad fate of the Yazidis. As Azar pointed out, any fool could see exactly where ISIS was headed in August 2014, but because the Yazidis existed outside the K.R.G. power structure, because they had no traditional alliance with either rival faction, they were left to largely fend for themselves. For all the excuses offered up by K.R.G. politicians and generals, the undeniable fact is that Sinjar simply wouldn't have happened if its residents had been named Barzani or Talabani.

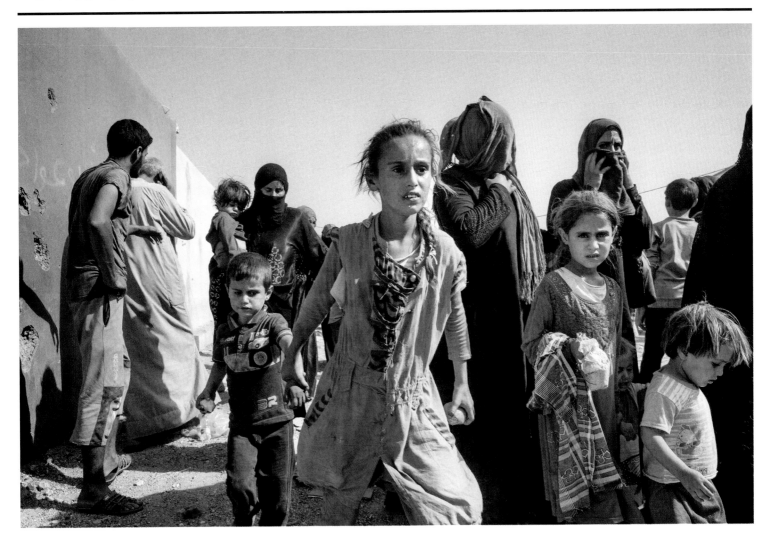

And what happens in the K.R.G. when the current danger subsides? If history is a guide, the Barzani-Talabani schism will worsen and may even lead to another civil war, for part of the hidden history of this place is the series of internecine battles the tribes have waged ever since they first came into contact, a legacy of mutual bloodletting dating back at least half a century and extending to as recently as the mid-1990s. It's a hidden history that the Mirkhan family knows from personal experience.

Over the course of many conversations with the various Mirkhan brothers, I heard a great deal about the exploits and personalities of the two family members who lost their lives as pesh merga and who have now entered the pantheon of Kurdish martyrs: their father, Heso, and their brother, Ali. What I heard little about — and the brothers' reticence on this topic became increasingly striking — were the actual circumstances of their deaths. It was only after repeated prodding that Azar finally divulged what I'd already ascertained independently: rather than by the Kurds' myriad external enemies, Heso and Ali Mirkhan were actually killed by rival Kurdish pesh merga.

"It's a disgrace that Kurds should kill each other," Azar offered when I asked why he'd been so reluctant to share the information. "With all the other enemies we have, how can we ever turn on each other?"

An excellent question, but it is one likely to be asked again all across a partitioned Middle East, no matter how far down those divisions and subdivisions are made.

At about the midpoint on the Sinjar plateau, a bend in the road suddenly revealed an exquisite village on the far side of the river: a series of houses climbing the rocky hillside and, just below them, a number of ancient stone terraces. Some of the terrace walls were more than 20 feet high, the inhabitants determined to carve out any little piece of workable land from the mountain and, built in an age before machines, must have taken years — decades, perhaps — to erect. The homes were deserted now, their roofs caved in by Saddam Hussein's soldiers, but they had left the terraces alone.

"It must have been so beautiful here then," Azar said, gazing up at the village, "a kind of garden."

But for Azar, the past was most useful for what it said about the future, and putting Sinjar behind us had set him in a happier, anticipatory mood. As we continued across Sinjar mountain, he drummed his fingers on the steering wheel.

"This is our time now," he said. "Iraq is gone. Syria is gone. Now it is our time." ◆

EPILOGUE

AFTER 16 MONTHS of traveling in the Middle East, I find it impossible to predict what might happen next, let alone sum up what it all means. In most every place Paolo Pellegrin and I went, the situation today looks worse than it did when we set out: The repression of the Sisi regime in Egypt has deepened; the war in Syria has taken tens of thousands more lives; to add to its other problems, Libya is now hurtling toward insolvency. If there is one bright spot on the map, it is the apparently solid and committed international coalition that is now working toward the final destruction of ISIS.

That said, I am reminded of something Majd Ibrahim told me: "ISIS isn't just an organization, it's an idea." It is also a kind of tribe, of course, and if this incarnation is destroyed, the conditions that created ISIS will remain in the form of a generation of disaffected and futureless young men, like Wakaz Hassan, who find purpose and power and belonging by picking up a gun. In short, nothing gets better anytime soon.

On a more philosophical level, this journey has served to remind me again of how terribly delicate is the fabric of civilization, of the vigilance required to protect it and of the slow and painstaking work of mending it once it has been torn. This is hardly an original thought; it is a lesson we were supposed to have learned after Nazi Germany, after Bosnia and Rwanda. Perhaps it is a lesson we need to constantly relearn.

Against this, I find solace in the extraordinary power of the individual to bring change, and no person that I met more exemplified this than Khulood al-Zaidi. Through sheer force of will, Khulood — the youngest daughter of a traditional family in a provincial city in Iraq — became an unlikely yet remarkable leader and in the process saved what she could of her family. Here, too, though, is a paradox: It is people like Khulood who must see to the mending of these fractured lands. Yet, it is those very people, the best their nations have to offer, who are leaving in search of a better life elsewhere. Today, Austria's gain is Iraq's loss.

As I write this, the Iraqis are slowly retaking cities from ISIS across the country's central plains: Ramadi was recaptured in February, Falluja in June. Planning for a joint offensive of Iraqi and Kurdish forces against Mosul is in its advanced stages, and the strike could come as early as October. One who will most certainly play a role in that offensive is Dr. Azar Mirkhan. For Azar, however, the true struggle, of fully separating his Kurdish homeland from the Arab world, will continue in the battle's aftermath. That aftermath will also mark the end of Wakaz Hassan's usefulness to his captors; as bluntly explained by the Kurdish security officer, he will then almost surely be handed over to Iraqi authorities for execution.

In Libya, Majdi el-Mangoush is continuing his engineering studies, but in contemplating the chaos engulfing his homeland, he has turned to a novel idea: a restoration of the monarchy that Qaddafi overthrew in 1969. "Not that it will solve all our problems," Majdi told me, "but at least with the king, we were a nation." Whatever happens in Libya, he is committed to staying and working for its improvement. "I am ready for a new kind of uncertainty," he said.

In Dresden, Majd Ibrahim has been granted refugee status, which will enable him to remain in Germany for at least the next three years. Now learning German, he hopes to return to college this fall for a master's degree in hotel management.

In Egypt, Laila Soueif's son, Alaa, is in the second year of his five-year prison sentence. Her daughter, Sanaa, was released in September 2015 under a presidential pardon, after having served 15 months. In May, though, she was found guilty of "insulting the judiciary" for failing to answer a prosecutor's request for an interview. Given a six-month sentence, Sanaa is currently being held at a women's prison in Cairo.

In Austria, Khulood and her sister Teamim continue to live with the Edelsbrunner family and were recently awarded scholarships to study intercultural management at a local university beginning in September. Not long ago, their mother, Aziza, who had never left Iraq, and whom Khulood had seen only once since she fled 11 years ago, died in Kut. Khulood's response to the news was typical of this dauntless young woman. She redoubled her efforts to rescue her remaining family, the father and sister still stranded in Jordan, and bring them to Austria. "To bring them here, to have a family again," she said. "That is my greatest dream." ◆

PLATES

Col. Muammar el-Qaddafi in Tripoli, Libya, October 2002.

Near Basra, Iraq, April 2003.

Near Basra, April 2003.

Near Ben Gardane, March 2011.

Near Ben Gardane, March 2011.

Azar Mirkhan at a front-line position in Sinjar, Iraq, March 2015.

A clash between Syrian and Afghan refugees in Mytilini, September 2015.

A Syrian collapsing in the heat in Mytilini, September 2015.

Refugees in Tikrit, Iraq, July 2016.

Near Tahrir Square in Cairo,
February 2011.

Near Tahrir Square, February 2011.

Refugees coming from Libya at the border
near Ben Gardane, Tunisia, March 2011.

Azar Mirkhan being shown ISIS-held positions
in and around Sinjar, May 2015.

Arbat, a refugee camp near
Sulaimaniya, Iraq, June 2015.

Refugees outside a police booth in
Mytilini, Greece, September 2015.

A camp for internally displaced
people in Baghdad, July 2016.

Tikrit, July 2016.

The New York Times Magazine